GLOBAL MOTHER TONGUE

Global
Mother Tongue

THE EIGHT FLAVOURS OF ENGLISH

Howard Richler

Véhicule Press

Published with the generous assistance of The Canada Council for the Arts,
the Book Publishing Industry Development Program of the Department of
Canadian Heritage (BPIDP), and the Société de développement des
entreprises culturelles du Québec (SODEC).

Cover design: J.W. Stewart
Set in Minion by Simon Garamond
Printed by Marquis Printing Inc.

LIBRARY AND ARCHIVES CANADA CATALOGUING IN PUBLICATION

Richler, Howard, 1948-
Global mother tongue : the eight flavours of English / Howard Richler.
ISBN 1-55065-215-X

1. English language—Dialects. 2. English language—Variation.
3. English language—Foreign elements. I. Title.

PE1074.7.R53 2006   427   C2006-902375-1

Published by Véhicule Press, Montréal, Québec, Canada
www.vehiculepress.com

Distribution in Canada: LitDistCo orders@litdistco.ca
Distribution USA: Independent Publishers Group
www.ipgbook.com

Printed and bound in Canada on 100% post-consumer recycled paper.

ANCIENT FOREST
FRIENDLY

To Phyllis & Louis Richler

(Mom & Dad)

Contents

They have been at a great feast of languages,
and stolen the scraps.

–Moth, *Love's Labour Lost* v.1

Introduction

The title of a book that suggests that English is the "world's language" is bound to raise hackles in certain locales, one of them being the place where I live, Quebec. I am mindful of linguist David Crystal's caveat in the preface to *English as a Global Language* that books entitled like his and mine will probably be interpreted as political statements. However, I am merely paraphrasing the words of François Chevillet, professor of English at Université Stendhal in Grenoble, France: "L'anglais n'est pas une langue internationale, à l'instar de l'espagnol ou du russe, mais c'est une langue mondiale." This translates as, "English is not an international language like Spanish or Russian, but a world language." By dichotomizing between Spanish, Russian, and, in effect, French as "international" languages, and English as the only "world" language, Chevillet sets it apart not only from all the other major languages in the world, but also from all languages in the course of history. While a language such as Chinese has many more first-language speakers than English, there are not too many people on this planet who speak Chinese as a second language. However, on most parts of the globe one can expect to find people who are conversant in English.

Why is this?

In *Hamlet*, perhaps the greatest work of English literature, Polonius advises his son Laertes, "Neither a borrower nor a lender be." While this may be solid paternal advice, it does not describe the course that the English language has taken.

In many cases, for example, we have received a culinary bonus. All the following have expanded our vocabulary in this century, while enriching our palates. Around 1900 "chop suey" joined our lexicon from Chinese; in the 1910s we got "shish kebab" from Turkish. In the 1920s, "sukiyaki" and "tempura" were absorbed from Japanese, "samogon" from Russian, "scampi" and "zucchini" from Italian, and "haute cuisine" from French. The importation of foreign food terms into our language increased dramatically in the 1930s. "Bagel" and "knish" arrived from Yiddish; "pesto," "pizza," "antipasto," and "tortellini" from Italian; "burrito" from Spanish;

"cassoulet" and "coq au vin" from French, and "satay" from Indonesian. The 1940s added "feta" and "moussaka" from Greek (originally from Egyptian Arabic); "linguine" and "manicotti" from Italian; "quiche" from French; "taco" from Spanish; "pastrami" from Rumanian and "won ton" and "dim sum" from Chinese. The 1950s were graced by "souvlaki" from Greek, "hummus" from Turkish, "tandoori" and "tikka" from Hindi, and "falafel" from Arabic. The 1960s added "teriyaki" and "rumaki" from Japanese, "ossobuco" from Italian, and "crudité" from French. "Nouvelle cuisine" is a neologism of the 1970s from French, as is "calzone" from Italian. In the 1980s we added "penne," "focaccia," "bruschetta," "frittata," "cannoli," "latte," and "tiramisu" from Italian, "chimichanga" and "fajita" from Spanish, "nan" bread from Hindi, "baba ghanouj" from Arabic, "bok choy" from Chinese, and "tzaziki" from Greek.

For centuries English has been raiding other languages for words. The nice thing about this type of larceny is that it enriches the borrower without impoverishing the lender.

The English language has accumulated by far the largest vocabulary in the world, yet studies show no more than 30 per cent of English words derive from the original Anglo-Saxon word stock. There are probably as many words of French origin as Anglo-Saxon origin in English. Sometimes it feels that English is nothing more than poorly pronounced French. Yet unlike the French who anguish incessantly about anglicisms, you don't hear too many murmurs about the galling gallicisms that pervade our language.

For the French the equation of language to culture is an important cornerstone of language policy. In English, on the other hand, there is less of a cultural component tied to learning the language, so you can learn it without the implicit message that you must adopt a new set of values. This is one reason why English seems more open to the acquisition of new speakers than French.

Also, unlike other languages, there is not the sense that there is a definitive way of speaking English. Although there are two main forms, American and British, English is spoken everywhere in the world to some degree. In fact, there are more speakers of English in India and Pakistan than in England! English is not tied to any particular social, political, economic, or religious system, or to any specific racial or cultural group. English belongs to no one and to everyone. And why not? It has borrowed from everyone.

Moreover, particularly in the 20th century the English language has become a large exporter of words to other languages. In Korea, people will say "apar" for apartment and "interior" for interior design. In Germany, a handsome youth may tell you proudly that he's a "Dressman." This does not mean that he's a transvestite, but a male model. Similarly in France, liking "foot" is not some bizarre fetish but refers to a love of football, whereas in Spain "footing" means jogging!

Unlike the hospitable reception foreign words receive upon entering the English language, however, these "anglicisms" are often viewed as pernicious invaders, and in some quarters as virtual agents of Anglo-American imperialism.

We have never felt that borrowing words from other languages could hurt English. Throughout its history, the English language has willingly accepted words from other languages with which it has been in contact.

Of all major languages, English is the only one that has avoided having a language academy to "protect" its language. Robert Claiborne in *Our Marvellous Native Tongue* states that "If borrowing foreign words could destroy a language, English would be dead (borrowed from Old Norse), deceased (from French), defunct (from Latin), and kaput (from German)."

The English language is one of the growth industries of the world. English is the mother tongue of over 350 million people. (*World Almanac and Ethnologue* cites as many as 450 million mother-tongue speakers of English.) At present there are in addition at least that many fluent second-language speakers of English. It has been calculated that 1.6 billion people have acquired at least a limited knowledge of English. This represents almost one-third of the planet's population. Because of much higher birth rates in developing parts of the world, it is calculated that by the year 2025 there will be substantially more second-language speakers of English than first-language speakers.

As English becomes the world's first true lingua franca (in the sense that it is spoken everywhere on the globe), a book that celebrates the international flavour of the global language is a necessity. This is one of my purposes in writing *Global Mother Tongue*.

English is going through a breathtaking process of change as lexicographic resources are finally able to document the global resource called English. Among other things, I want to explore the process of how English absorbed, and continues to absorb, so many words from so many languages.

Borrowing is one of myriad factors that are changing our language. Why has English been more prepared than other languages to be a language borrower? Why aren't we English-speakers overly concerned that foreign words will corrupt our language?

1

The Global Language

In the closing years of the 20th century, the English language has become a global resource. As such, it does not owe its existence or the
protection of its essence to any nation or group. Inasmuch as a particular language belongs to any individual or community, English is
the possession of every individual and every community that in any
way uses it, regardless of what any other individual or community may
think or feel about the matter.
        −*The Oxford Companion to the English Language*

Even Fidel Castro has thrown in the towel. He stated at a conference of
Caribbean countries held in the Dominican Republic in 1998 that
"globalization is an inevitable process. It would be pointless to oppose a
law of history." And the verdict is in: English has become the world's global
language.

This is a relatively new development. Linguist David Crystal begins
the preface to *English as a Global Language* by stating that "in 1950, any
notion of English as a true world language was but a dim ... possibility,
surrounded by the political uncertainty of the Cold War, and lacking any
clear definition or sense of direction."

To listen to the musings of some language commentators, you'd think
that this has happened by virtue of the superiority of English. In 1848 in
the British periodical *The Athenaeum* a reviewer opined, "In the easiness
of grammatical construction, in its paucity of inflections, in its almost
total disregard of the distinctions of gender, ... in the simplicity and
precision of its terminations and auxiliary verbs, ... our mother-tongue
seems well adapted by organization to become the language of the world."

A century or so later, Robert Claiborne in *Our Marvellous Native Tongue*
writes, "Can I really be claiming that English is not merely a great language
but the greatest? Yes, that's exactly what I'm saying."

Richard Lederer writes in *The Miracle of Language* that "English possesses
a fairly simple, stripped-down apparatus of grammar, unencumbered by
complex nouns and adjective inflections and gender markers."

15

I have developed a university course entitled "Mastering English," targeted to language students; many have agreed that English is among the easiest languages to learn because of its relatively simple grammatical structure.

It is not only anglophones who extol the virtues of the English language. In an article entitled *"L'anglais, langue paradoxale"* in the Parisian newspaper *Courrier International* in September 2005, Jean-Claude Sergeant, *professeur de civilisation britanique* at the University of Paris, praised English for both its suppleness and its inherent "no-nonsense" nature.

Nonetheless, one can easily point to facets of English that make it difficult to learn. It is highly idiomatic and therefore illogical. Its pronunciation and spelling seem haphazard. It abounds with homonyms. Some of them—such as "cleave," "sanction," and "scan"—even have diametrically opposite meanings.

Perhaps non-linguistic factors help to account for the globalization of English. Roger Lass argues in *The Shape of English* that it is not the "superiority of a language that hastens its spread, but other factors: (a) the extent to which it is imposed as a colonial language on non-speakers, (b) the extent to which it is of economic utility to non-speakers to learn it, and (c) the extent to which access to the language means access to a culture felt to be in some way a necessary, useful or prestigious possession." David Crystal echoes this: "A language becomes an international language for one chief reason: the political power of its people—especially their military power." Crystal adds that "it may take a militarily powerful nation to establish a language, but it takes an economically powerful one to maintain and expand it." Not only does money talk, it also tends to converse in the language of the nation with the most powerful currency.

Not to be underestimated is the widespread view of the world's youth that English is a "cool" language. Artists whose mother tongue is not English are recording songs in English because of the dominance of the language on the international popular music scene. The most popular movies in the world are in English. It is not unusual nowadays to hear about an Italian, Spanish, or French director making a movie in English.

All these factors motivate people. Individuals involved in second-language instruction have consistently told me that the key ingredient is not the teacher's method but the motivation of the student. People are likely to be motivated to learn our language because of the international flavour of our vocabulary. Teachers of English as a second language (ESL) have mentioned to me that students frequently relate that a certain English word they're learning comes from their mother tongue. Even with its grammatical irregularity and illogical pronunciation, English is well suited to be the world's common means of communication because it is arguably the most welcoming, absorbent, and adaptable language in the world. The English language is like a harbour with words floating like ships from abroad carrying exotic messages to our shores.

Sixteenth-century educator Richard Mulcaster vigorously defended borrowing new words into English. He argued that English acquires new words not only out of "necessitie" but also out of mere "braverie to garnish itself withal." His confrère George Pettie noted that borrowing was "the ready way to inrich our tongue and make it copious." Because of this welcoming tendency, English has accumulated by far the world's largest, and perhaps its most varied and expressive, vocabulary, with more than double the words of its nearest competitors, German, French, and Russian.

Two examples display the variety of choices we have in English: the verb "say" and the adjective "fast." Some of the options for "say" are: "assert," "affirm," "predicate," "enunciate," "state," "declare," "profess," "aver," "avouch," "put forth," "advance," "express," "allege," "pose," "propose," "propound," "broach," "maintain," "contend," "pronounce," "speak," "tell," "utter," "speechify," "harangue," and "talk." For the adjective "fast" we have such synonyms as "speedy," "swift," "rapid," "quick," "fleet," "prompt," "expeditious," "hasty," "precipitate," and "mercurial."

Perhaps we should think in terms of Englishes, rather than English. There are varieties of English, with distinctive vocabulary, pronunciation, and in some cases even distinct grammar.

In Caribbean English if you've seen a "duppy" you've seen a ghost. Some usages are restricted to certain islands. If you're lucky in Jamaica, somebody might "sweetmouth" (flatter) you, and in St. Vincent people are "touchous," not touchy. In East Africa you don't become gluttonous but "foodious," and in West Africa you don't remove someone from authority, you "destool" them. In Nigeria it's more likely that someone will refer to the "outgone" president than the past president. In the Philippines you don't get assaulted by an armed robber but by a "holder-upper" and you might go to jail if you practice "estafa," which is "fraud" in Standard

English. If people in South Asia say they're going to send you their "biodata," they'll be forwarding their CVs. If you're on an English-language Internet site called "India World," an icon labeled "samachar" will lead you to current events. One called "dhan" will direct you towards investment information, and one called "khel" will take you to cricket news. In India, English-speaking people having a "masala" are having a casual conversation, and a grave mistake might be called a "Himalayan blunder." In Pakistan, an "earring" is an "eartop." In Singapore and Malaysia, a tired English-speaking worker might say, "I was blur at work." "Blur" means "not knowing what's going on."

Even some of the terms in the more standard Englishes might not be understood everywhere. In Australia a "paddock" is a field, and if someone asks you where the "dunny" is, they're looking for the toilet. If they call you a "wowser," they mean you're a wet blanket; the term refers to a puritanical person who disapproves of dancing and drinking. In New Zealand you don't attend a funeral but a "tangi" and you don't become frantic but "drissy." In Scotland arson might be referred to as "fire-raising" and in Ireland an "atomy" man would be an insignificant man.

In Malaysia, English-speakers use "similar" for "identical." In parts of the Caribbean "lunch" means an "afternoon snack" or "afternoon tea." In South Asia a "hotel" means "restaurant," but in some non-urban parts of Australia it can mean a "place that serves alcohol." In Ireland, "glow" can mean "noise" and "backward" can mean "shy." In India, "intermarriage" refers not only to people of different religions getting hitched but also to people from different castes. In Hong Kong, an "astronaut" can refer to a spouse semi-permanently in transit between Hong Kong and Vancouver or elsewhere.

It's helpful to think of our language as coming in eight flavours—African, American, Australian/New Zealand, British, Canadian, Caribbean, East Asian, and South Asian—each of which can be subdivided.

The *Oxford English Dictionary* (*OED*) demonstrates how new Englishes are altering the landscape of the language. The *OED*'s 1989 Second Edition was comprised of twenty-three volumes. When the Third Edition is published in 2010 it will have over forty volumes, with many of the new additions coming from the new Englishes. The sheer size of the *OED* has required it to go online.

Population trends indicate that within fifty years there will be at least 50

AFRICAN

Kenyan English
Nigerian English
South African English
West African Pidgin

AMERICAN

Black American Vernacular
Midland English
Northern English
Southern English

AUSTRALIAN
& NEW ZEALAND

Aboriginal English
Australian English
New Zealand English
Tok Pisin

BRITISH

English English
Irish English
Scottish English
Welsh English

CANADIAN

Athabaskan English
Inuit English
Newfoundland English
Quebec English

CARIBBEAN

Bahamian English
Barbadian English
Jamaican English
Trinidadian English

EAST ASIAN

Hong Kong English
Malaysian English
Philippines English
Singapore English

SOUTH ASIAN

Bangladeshi English
Indian English
Pakistani English
Sri Lankan English

per cent more second-language English speakers than first-language speakers.

This has important usage implications. Just to give one example, in Standard English the usage "I am knowing" is not acceptable. This usage, however, is perfectly acceptable in Indian English.

This trend does not always sit well with all the originators of the English language—the English. Prince Charles, for example, has complained about the corrupting tendencies of non-British English. He'd like the British version to lead the way as the world language. In understated Queen's English, the Prince of Wales averred, "I think we have to be a bit careful, otherwise the whole thing could get rather a mess."

With all due respect to Prince Charles, if we didn't have these corrupting influences English would be impoverished. In any case, the English language ceased to be the sole possession of the English some time ago. Even the country with the largest number of English speakers, the United States, accounts for only 20 per cent of the world's English speakers. Peoples who were once colonized by the language are now rapidly domesticating it, remaking it, and becoming more and more relaxed about the way they use it.

A look at some of the recent winners of the Man Booker Prize highlights the international nature of contemporary English. The Man Booker Prize is the literary version of the Academy Awards. Each year it is awarded to what is deemed to be the best English-language novel written by a resident of the United Kingdom, the Commonwealth, or South Africa. Since 1980, these are some the countries where the winners were weaned: India (3 winners), Canada (3), Australia (4), New Zealand (1), Nigeria (1), Japan (1), Egypt (1), South Africa (2), Ireland (2), Scotland (1), and Sri Lanka (1). Some of the winners' backgrounds are hard to pin down. The 1992 co-winner, Michael Ondaatje, was characterized in a 1993 *Time* magazine article as a "Sri Lankan of Indian, Dutch and English ancestry, educated in Britain, long resident in Canada, with siblings on four continents." The same article goes on to say that "five days earlier the Nobel Prize for Literature was awarded to Derek Walcott, a poet of African, Dutch and English descent, born in St. Lucia and commuting these days between Boston and Trinidad." Yann Martel, the 2002 winner for *Life of Pi*, was born in Salamanca, Spain, of Canadian parents, but grew up in Costa Rica, France, Spain, and Mexico, in addition to Canada. The most recent winner,

Kiran Desai, was born in India in 1971, and educated in India, England, and the United States. She travels between the three countries, and is in on record as saying that she feels "no alienation or dislocation."

A fundamental aspect of this flexible situation is that the rise of Englishes permits expression of different insights and perspectives, and enables people to attain a more profound understanding of the human mind and soul. Ironically, in many places the English language is fulfilling both functions. Singaporean novelist Catherine Lim stated that "I need Singlish [Singapore English] to express a Singaporean feeling."

The price of having a world language is tolerance and an appreciation for its myriad flavours. Non-native speakers of English share the sense of ownership in the global language.

According to Jamaican writer Mervyn Morris, "One values greatly the Creole because it expresses things about the Jamaican experience which are not available for expressions in the same force in Standard English." Proficiency in Standard English, however, is important to Morris, "because we do not want … to cut ourselves off from international communication."

Some see the devotion of some writers to the language of their former oppressors as a source of angst. But there is another way of looking at this; according to the *Time* article, writers such as Walcott have used "English as a way to reclaim a heritage, and to take the instrument of imperialism and turn it upon itself."

2

The Conflict Over Purity

Usually a language is dominated by its élites. In these circumstances, language serves as a shibboleth, a badge marking membership in the upper rank of society, and there is a tendency to elaborate rules which may make the language more complex. But after the Norman conquest of England in 1066, there was no longer an English-speaking elite. French was the language of the ruling class and the language of high culture, while English became a vernacular spoken by peasants. For about two centuries English almost ceased being used as a written language.

And it was just as well. While spoken Old English had lost most of its inflections by the time of the Norman Invasion, this was not the case with written English. By the time documents started to be recorded again on a regular basis in English in the 13th century, inflections were also absent from the written language.

Probably more important than actual changes to English was the fact that active control of English had been wrested from the hands of the elites. Although by the 14th century there was a resurgence in pride in the English language and knowledge of French was waning in Britain, English was by no means a status language. Even into the 16th century, it was regarded as a second-rate literary language. When Thomas More published *Utopia* in 1516, he published it not in English but in Latin. It would not be until 1551 that the book was published in English; by then it had already been translated into French, German, and Italian. Some 16th-century commentators objected strenuously to the use of English as a scholarly language. They felt that English could never compare to the standards of Latin or Greek, especially in such fields as theology or medicine. These purists never garnered much support. One person who was key in the campaign against the English dissers was educator Richard Mulcaster, who said: "For is it not in dede a marvellous bondage, to become servant to one tung for learning sake, the most of our time, whereas we maie have the verie same treasur in our own tung, with the gain of most time? Our own bearing the joyfull title to our libertie and freedom, the Latin tung remembering us of our thraldom and bondage? I love Rome, but London better; I favor Italie, but England more; I honor the Latin, but I worship the English."

The Mulcaster position triumphed. Latin continued to be used by certain scientists into the 16th century, but went out of use by the 17th century, apart from its liturgical use by the Church.

Of course, English was not indifferent to the beauty of Latin and Greek, and during the Renaissance it adopted countless words from the classical languages. Here is a sampling: "absurdity," "agile," "alienate," "assassinate," "autograph," "catastrophe," "chaos," "climax," "disrespect," "emphasis," "encyclopedia," "enthusiasm," "epilepsy," "exaggerate," "exist," "expensive," "external," "fact," "habitual," "halo," "harass," "idiosyncrasy," "immaturity," "jocular," "larynx," "lexicon," "lunar," "monopoly," "monosyllable," "necessitate," "obstruction," "pancreas," "parenthesis," "pathetic," "pneumonia," "relaxation," "relevant," "skeleton," "species," "system," "tendon," "thermometer," "tibia," "transcribe," "ulna," "utopian," "vacuum," and "virus."

It was probably because English had absorbed so many words from French thanks to its Norman conquerors that it was receptive to borrowings from other languages. It is perhaps instructive that English, of all European languages, is the only one that has never established a language academy to "protect" it from foreign incursions.

Given this openness to change, it is not surprising that when written literary English started to blossom in the 16th century, the mindset of Elizabethan writers was to accept all sorts of verbal wealth. They were not restricted by thoughts of rendering English impure and if they knew of a word from another tongue, they would gleefully adopt it. Writers were conditioned to think outside the box because nobody was really sure what constituted the rules of English writing. Shakespeare was fortunate to be living at a time when the English language was very fluid. This enabled him to do what he liked with English; it had no fixed rules and he drew power and beauty from its fluidity.

William Styron in *Sophie's Choice* highlights the expressiveness of English in a passage where the heroine, Polish-born Sophie, expresses mock horror at the variety of English words:

> "Such a language! ... Too many words. I mean just the word for *vélocité*. I mean 'fast.' 'Rapid.' 'Quick.' All the same thing! A scandal!"

" 'Swift,' " I added.

"How about 'speedy'?" Nathan said.

" 'Hasty,' " I went on.

"And 'fleet,' " Nathan said, "though that's a bit fancy."

" 'Snappy!' " I said.

"Stop it!" Sophie said, laughing. "Too much! Too many words, this English. In French it is so simple, you just say '*vite*.' "

The reason English offers so many choices is that in many cases we have a three-tiered vocabulary of synonyms from Anglo-Saxon, French, and classical Greek and Latin that affords us at least three choices when we're searching for *le mot juste*.

Words that we take from other languages often acquire extended meanings in their English environs. The word "*karma*" in Sanskrit means fate. In English, it has acquired the sense of an "aura of good or bad emanating from a person." Similarly, the word "blitz" (from "*blitzkrieg*") which referred in World War II to a sudden overpowering bombardment, acquired a football sense in the 1960s. "*Honcho*" in Japanese means "squad leader," while in English, it has acquired the sense of "boss" and is starting to be used as a verb meaning "to oversee." Increasingly, I also hear the German-bred noun "angst" being rendered verb-like in the form of "angsting."

In addition, foreign borrowings may acquire narrowed meanings. Take two Mexican foods, "tacos" and "enchiladas." In Mexico, "taco" refers to anything rolled in a tortilla, but in most English contexts a taco is a crisply fried tortilla filled with a spicy ground-beef mixture. Similarly, in Mexico "enchilada" refers to anything covered in chili or ground pepper. In North America, however, "enchilada" refers to a corn tortilla prepared in a specific manner.

Before the demise of the Soviet Union, Russian journalist Vladimir Vasilyev wrote an article deploring how the Russian language had become polluted by the adoption of anglicisms such as "*boss*," "*referee*," "*offis*," "*servis*," and "*plantsiya*" (plantation). Ironically, none of these words are "pure" English. "Boss" comes from Dutch, "referee," "office," and "service" from French, and "plantation" from Latin. In Quebec, French "purists" have insisted that road signs be marked with "*arrêt*" instead of "stop," notwithstanding that "stop" was originally borrowed by the English from French. Similar complaints have been made about anglicisms such as "rosbif" ("roast beef") and "check" that were taken from the French.

English Synonyms with Anglo-Saxon, French, and Greek or Latin Roots

ANGLO-SAXON	FRENCH	GREEK/LATIN
ask	question	interrogate
big	large	voluminous
dead	deceased	defunct
eat	devour	consume
end	finish	conclude
fair	beautiful	attractive
fast	firm	secure
fear	terror	trepidation
goodness	virtue	probity
help	aid	assist
holy	sacred	consecrated
house	residence	domicile
kingly	royal	regal
rise	mount	ascend
say	declare	attest
small	puny	minuscule
thin	spare	emaciated
time	age	epoch
work	labour	exertion
write	compose	inscribe

The French work from a different conception of language. Some years ago while on a trip to China, former French prime minister Lionel Jospin stated that the "English language will be used by everyone and will lose its original beauty, while French ... will retain its purity." The notion of a pure language, however, is as fictitious as the concept of a pure race. The French word for language, "*langue*," takes the feminine gender, and if truth be known, the lady was never pure. In *The Roots of Language* Claiborne points out that "French was long ago corrupted by borrowings from Gaulic and Germanic and later Italian, Spanish, and Arabic."

The French have long been concerned with protecting their beloved language from corrupting influences. In 1635, *L'Académie française* was established under the auspices of Cardinal Richelieu. Its mandate was "to labour with all possible care and diligence to give definite rules to language and to render it pure, eloquent and capable of treating the arts and sciences." Forty academicians were drawn from the ranks of the church, nobility, and military—a bias which exists to the present day. Knowledge about language has never been a criterion for inclusion in this august body. Not only has less than 50 per cent of its membership been writers, but also in the whole history of *L'Académie française* there have only been two philologists. The first *académicienne* was not elected until 1981.

The French were not the first European country to establish a language academy to safeguard their mother tongue. That distinction is owned by Italy; Italians established the *Accademia della Crusca* in 1572 with the intent of purifying Italian. In 1617 the *Fruchtbringende Gesellschaft* was established in Germany by Ludwig of Anhalt-Köthen, who was himself a member of the Italian academy. Several other European nations established language academies in the 18th and 19th centuries. The Spanish Academy was founded in 1713, and within the next two hundred years corresponding regulatory agencies were established in most South American Spanish-speaking countries. Sweden had its language academy by 1786, Hungary in 1830. There are Arabic language academies in Egypt, Iraq, and Syria, and Israel established the Hebrew Language Academy in 1953.

There have been calls to cleanse English of impurities. In 1557, John Cheke sent a letter to Thomas Hoby in which he said, "I am of this opinion that our tung shold be written cleane and pure, unmixt and umangeled with borrowing of other tunges." Such public declarations about the corruption of English, however, are not common.

A proposal for an academy was made in England in the 18th century; it had proponents of the caliber of John Dryden, Joseph Addison, and later on, Daniel Defoe, but it never got off the ground. In 1708 Defoe penned, "an Englishman has his mouth full of borrow'd phrases. ... He is allways borrowing other men's languages. ... I cannot but think the using and introducing foreign terms of art or foreign words is an intolerable grievance." In 1712 Jonathan Swift presented his *Proposal for Correcting, Improving and Ascertaining the English Tongue* in which he lamented to the Earl of Oxford, "Our language is extremely imperfect; that its daily improvements are by no means in proportion to its daily corruptions; that the pretenders to polish ... it have chiefly multiplied abuses and absurdities; and that in many instances it offends against every part of grammar." Swift hoped to "fix our language for ever," and said that it was preferable for a language "not to be wholly perfect, than it should be perpetually changing."

When Samuel Johnson began his dictionary project thirty years later, his original intention was to follow the philosophy proposed by Swift. Like French lexicographers, Johnson believed that all language change is evil. But by 1755, when his dictionary was finally published, he had come to realize that a language was either alive and uncontrollable, or stable and therefore dead. He had also concluded that the attempts by the Italians and French to control language were futile:

> Academies have been instituted to guard the avenues of ... language, to retain fugitives, and to repulse intruders, but their vigilance and activity have hitherto been vain; sounds are too volatile and subtle for legal restraints; to enchain syllables, and to lash the wind, are equally the undertakings of pride, unwilling to measure its desires by its strengths.

In the preface to his *Dictionary*, Johnson wrote,

> When we see men grow old and die at a certain time ... we laugh at the elixir that promises to prolong life ... and with equal justice may the lexicographer be derided, who being able to produce no example of a nation that has preserved their words and phrases from mutability, shall imagine that his dictionary can embalm his language, and secure it from corruption, and decay, that it is in his power to change sublunary nature, or clear the world at once from folly, vanity and affectation.

There have been English purists who wanted to return English to its Anglo-Saxon roots. Some 19th-century British poets actually prepared a list of "purer" English words, such as "starkin" (from the German "*strenchen*") instead of "asterisk"; "gainsay" instead of "contradict"; "withstand" instead of "resist"; "lawcraft" instead of "jurisprudence"; "talecraft" instead of "arithmetic"; "wortlore" instead of "botany"; "starcraft" instead of "astronomy"; "fireghost" instead of "electricity"; "faith-heat" instead of "enthusiasm," and "midding" instead of "mediocre." Once again, these proposals fell on deaf English ears.

Francophone elites are more inclined to the poets' than to the lexicographers' *Weltanschauung*. The French have opposed borrowings from other languages, and not only those from English. German chemical terminology that pervaded English in the early part of the 20th century was vigorously denounced by French elites, for example. For centuries they have resisted wave after corrupting wave of linguistic imperialism. Associations have been established in France to stem the corrupting tides. In addition to the *Académie*, *L'Office de la langue française* was founded in 1937, *La Comité d'Étude des termes techniques français* in 1954, and *L'Office du vocabulaire français* in 1957. None of these institutions have proved particularly successful in their efforts. Steven Pinker says the purpose of *L'Académie française* is "to amuse journalists from other countries with bitterly argued decisions that the French gaily ignore." Latest on the list of dreaded anglicisms are terms coming from the connected fields of technology and finance. "E-mail" is to be eschewed in favor of "*courrier électronique*" or "*courriel*;" "start-up" should be rendered as "*jeune pousse*" ("young plant"), and a "stock option" becomes "*une option sur titre*."

Linguistic matters are taken just as seriously in Quebec. In April 1999, L'Office québécois de la langue française (OLF), the guardian of French chastity in Quebec, issued a twenty-seven-page booklet that allowed French-speaking golfers to play purely in French. Not since the early 1980s when the OLF tried to feed us "*hambourgeoise*" ("hamburger") and "*boeuf mariné*" ("smoked meat") has our plate been so full. With a proper *léger crochet de droite* ("fade") or *léger crochet de gauche* ("draw") you might get a *oiselet* ("birdie") presuming you don't hit a *crochet de gauche* ("hook") or *éclisse* ("slice") and land up in deep *broussaille* ("rough"). If your ball gets ensconced in a *fosse de sable* ("sand trap"), you'll be lucky to escape with a "*boguey*," notwithstanding that the word "bogey" is eponymous.

According to the *OED*,

> One popular song at least has left its permanent effect on the game of golf. That song is "The Bogey Man." In 1890 Dr. Thomas Browne, R.N., the honourary secretary of the Great Yarmouth Club, was playing against a Major Wellman, the match being against the "ground score," which was the name given to the scratch value of each hole. The system of playing against the "ground score" was new to Major Wellman, and he exclaimed, thinking of the song of the moment, that his mysterious and well-nigh invincible opponent was a regular "bogey-man." The name "caught on" at Great Yarmouth, and today "Bogey" is one of the most feared opponents on all the courses that acknowledge him.

American golfers preferred the term "par" to express the British meaning of "bogey" and thus transformed the term to refer to "one over par."

The French are imbued from birth with the belief that French is virtually a divine language. J. Harzic is quoted in Blancpain and Reboullet's *Le Français et les autres langues de communication*: "Les Français ont une conviction innée dans la supériorité de leur langue." ("The French have an innate conviction in the superiority of their language.") The quintessence of French perfection was glorified by Count Antoine de Rivarol in 1784:

> There has never been a language in which you could write more purely and more precisely than in ours, which is more resistant to equivocations and every kind of obscurity, more serious and more gentle at the same time, more suitable for all kinds of styles, purer in its phrases, more judicious in its expressions, which has a greater liking for elegance and ornament, but which is more fearful of affectation.

These sentiments have been repeated time after time. In 1963, Gaullist J. Duron wrote: "I consider precision and clarity to be the prime quality of our language ... to such an extent that I doubt whether there has ever existed since the time of the Greeks, a language which reflected thought so transparently." Nor is such chauvinism the monopoly of the right-wing forces in France. Former Socialist President François Mitterrand stated, "On the subject of the French language, after so many others it is hard to add further praising words to those so often repeated concerning its rigour, its clarity, its elegance, its nuances, the richness of its tenses and its moods, the delicacy of its sounds, the logic of its word order." For the French nowadays, the *bête noire* is the English language. French philosopher Michel Serres once remarked that "there are more English words in the streets of Paris today than there were German words during the Nazi occupation."

The French feel that when their language is spread they must be vigilant that it doesn't encounter molestation. In the French view it is better that the language be acquired perfectly by the select few rather than imperfectly by the hordes likely to abuse it. To speak French badly, to break the rules of French grammar or to make frequent use of foreign words is to be unpatriotic in some manner. The French insist that they "own" French and the standards that are set must be made in the source country—France. It is a rare Frenchman who is willing to defend patois usages. In 1980 French politician Raymond Barre stated, "The first of the fundamental values of our civilization is the correct usage of our language. There is among young people a moral and civic virtue in the loyal practice of French."

Linguist Robert Hall defines linguistic purism as "considering one type of language (a given dialect, or the speech of a given social class or of a certain epoch) as 'purer' than and therefore 'superior' to other types." He characterizes it as the "struggle against neologisms, against the introduction into usage of loan and international words ... not based on a scientific study of the development tendencies of a given language and the activity of the people attempting to protect their native tongue from foreign influence."

Contrast this Gallic mindset with attitudes in the English-speaking world. As linguist J.A. Fishman has commented, "English is less loved but more used; French is more loved but less used." The prevailing view against calls for the establishment of an English language academy was expressed by the 18th-century grammarian Thomas Sheridan, who said that it was "unsuited to the genius of a free nation." There has never been a belief that English is a superior language that must be protected from lesser languages. The prevailing attitude is that English is a language to be used, not to be worshipped. If the language changes along the way, so be it. English has generally proved accepting of local varieties and standards. Although there are the dominant standards, British and American, there is a growing awareness that not only do other standards such as Australian, Canadian, and Indian varieties exist, but that they are valid and enriching parts to our language. Even those who dislike some of the chaotic varieties begrudgingly accept that this is the price one must pay to have a truly global language. Robert Claiborne observes that

> like any other language, English ultimately reflects the imagination and creativity of those who speak and write it. ... And though Anglo-American linguistic creativity is doubtless no more vigorous than that of many other peoples, it has operated with almost no inhibitions, while in other places it has too often been blocked by the upraised finger of official or scholarly authority.

I would argue that the borrowing from English has served to make French a more vigorous language with a greater wealth of synonyms. French is no less French because of borrowing from English, any more than English is less distinctively English because of its myriad borrowings from French. When a language absorbs words from another language, those words are incorporated into the grammatical structure of the new language. Here are some examples, provided to me by University of Ottawa linguist Shana Poplack: "*Je ne serai pas capable de coper avec,*" and "*Puis les parents ont jamais voulu qu'ils la dépluggent, mais elle est morte quand même là.*"

In Quebec, ironically, francophones have co-opted the English word "chum" to serve a valuable purpose. "*Chum*" is used in Quebec French to refer to someone you're living with, in a romantic context. I find the word less sophomoric sounding than "boyfriend" or "girlfriend" and less blatant than "lover." The term "partner" is confusing and the euphemistic "significant other" utterly absurd. English could use a word like "chum" to serve this purpose. I suggest we retaliate by co-opting the French "*co-vivant.*"

I think there are two main reasons for the different attitude towards purity in language displayed by the English. First, from 1066 to 1360 English wasn't the official language in England; French was the language of power. From 1250 to 1400, a huge number of French words swept into English from French. Normally the elites in a country would object to this foreign invasion, but in the case of England these elites were French-speaking. And even after English was re-established as the official language of the land, it was by no means a status language; well into the early part of the 16th century, many books in England would be first published in Latin, because English was thought to be an impoverished language. Also, from a practical point of view, when purists started to call for the expunging of the many foreign words (predominantly French and Latin) from our vocabulary, these words had been in common usage for too long and were entrenched and ensconced in our language. Even later in the 16th century when English was starting to flower as a written language, there was no strong prescriptive elite that could tell literary greats, such as Shakespeare, that it was improper to play with the language as they liked.

The second reason the English never feared an invasion of foreign words is because they were never invaded. Yes, the country was invaded in 1066, but at the time the modern concept of the nation had not emerged. Matters were dictated primarily by no more than the concept of different classes. The general absence of a fear of foreign domination by England after the Norman invasion helps explains why calls for a purification of the English language have always been muted.

There is another factor that has enhanced the willingness of English to be affected by foreign languages. Following the American War of Independence, there was a certain amount of antipathy towards the language of the American enemy in the war—the English. Some American patriots would have liked German, not English, to be established as the language of the new republic. This obviously was not feasible, as English was spoken by the vast majority of 18th-century Americans. In fact, in the early years of America, there seems to have been an extremely tolerant view towards language diversity. The constitution of the United States does not mention the English language. In 19th-century America, many different languages were spoken in the United States and there was not much ado about the widespread systems of education in languages other than English. There was a greater willingness in the United States to accept foreign terms than there was in England.

3

A Borrowed Language

I can't decide if I'm amused or bemused when I read a story about "the rape of German by English" or "the assault of anglicisms in Poland," because if ever there was a language that has been assaulted by another language, it is English by French. *Mon Dieu!* We're not even a Romance language and we must endure so many galling Gallicisms! But although English seems to prefer borrowing words from French over other languages, it has taken some words from virtually every language on the globe.

Let's examine our foreign bounty. Here is a list of over one hundred languages and a contribution from each language to our burgeoning lexicon. Where the word is somewhat obscure, the definition or source is given in brackets.

Abenaki: moose
Afrikaans: apartheid
Akan: okra
Albanian: lek (a unit of currency in Albania)
Algonquian: caucus
Amharic: madoqua (a tiny antelope of Ethiopia, of about the size of a hare)
Angolan: gumbo
Arabic: algebra
Araucanian: poncho
Arawak: iguana
Aramaic: Kol Nidre (a prayer, opening with the words *Kol nidhr*, sung by Jews at the beginning of the service on the eve of Yom Kippur)

Armenian: vartabed (a member of an order of clergy in the Armenian church)

Balinese: subak (a Balinese rice-growers' co-operative, organized to ensure equitable distribution of water for irrigation)
Basque: jai alai
Bengali: jute
Beothuk: mamateek (a wigwam of the Beothuk Indians)
Breton: bijou
Bulgarian: bugger
Burmese: petwood

Cantonese: typhoon
Carib: canoe

Catalan: paella
Chinook Jargon: muck-a-muck
Choctaw: bayou
Coptic: oasis
Cornish: killas (Cornish miners'
  term for clay-slate)
Cree: toboggan
Croatian: cravat
Czech: robot

Dakota: teepee
Danish: skill
Dharak: wombat
Dippil: koala
Djingulu: maluka (the person in
  charge; the boss)
Dutch: poppycock

Estonian: manna-croup (a coarse
  granular meal)

Fang: ovangkol (a leguminous tree
  indigenous to West Africa and
  western central Africa)
Finnish: sauna
Flemish: ghost
Fon: voodoo
French: nuance
French (Canadian): depanneur
  (a convenience store)
Frisian: boor
Fulani: mojo

Gaelic: bard
Galibi: divi-divi (a small tropical
  American tree with long seed
  pods)

German: angst
Greek: partridge
Guarani: cougar
Guugu Ymidhirr: kangaroo

Haitian: barbecue
Hausa: bogus (according to
  Barnhart and Metcalf in
  America in So Many Words)
Hawaiian: ukulele
Hindi: pundit
Hebrew: messiah
Hopi: kiva (a chamber, built
  wholly or partly underground,
  used by the male Pueblo Indians
  for religious rites)
Hungarian: coach

Icelandic: window
Igbo: okra
Indonesian: satay
Inuit: igloo
Irish: banshee
Italian: ballot
Japanese: karate
Javanese: batik
Kanarese: bamboo
Kekchi: kelep (a Central American
  stinging ant)
Khoisan: gnu
Kikongo: goober
Kimbundu: banjo
Kongo: zombie
Korean: tae kwon do
Kurdish: Kermanji (a language of
  the Iranian group spoken by the
  Kurds of Kurdistan)

Lapp: lemming
Latin: penis
Luo: nyatiti (musical instrument with eight strings resembling a lyre played by the Luo people of Kenya)

Malagasay: raffia (a type of palm)
Malay: amok
Malayalam: calico
Mande: banana
Mandingo: jazz (according to Smitherman in *Black Talk*)
Maori: kiwi
Marathi: mongoose
Maya: cenote (a natural underground reservoir of water, such as occurs in the limestone of Yucatán)
Mbuba: okapi (small giraffe-like animal native to Zaire)
Melanesian: taboo
Micmac: caribou

Nahuatl: peyote
Narragansett: moccasin
Navajo: hogan (a hut of Navajo and other American Indian peoples of the southwestern United States)
Nepali: rana (the title used by members of the family that virtually ruled Nepal from 1846 to 1951)
Nguni: lobola (the South African native custom of marriage by purchase)

Nootka: potlatch (a gift)
Norse (Old): skirt
Norwegian: fjord
Nyanja: kungu (a small East African gnat)
Nyungar: wilgie (a kind of red ochre used by Aborigines as a body paint)

Ojibwa: chipmunk

Persian: bazaar
Polish: mazurka
Portuguese: palaver
Prakrit: ginger
Provençal: jambalaya
Punjabi: kirpan (a sword or dagger worn by Sikh males as a religious symbol)

Quechuan: llama

Romany: pal
Russian: commissar
Rwandan: Mwami (a monarch in either of the former African kingdoms of Ruanda and Urundi)

Samoan: lava-lava (in Samoa and some other Pacific islands, a sort of skirt)
Sanskrit: swastika
Salish: sasquatch
Scots: kerfuffle
Serbo-Croatian: slivovitz
Shawnee: wapiti

Sinhalese: beriberi
Sioux: Miniconjou (a member of a division of the Teton Sioux people, inhabiting the Cheyenne River area of western South Dakota)
Sotho (Northern): Modjani (the Rain Queen)
Sotho (Southern): Ntate (a respectful form of address to an older man)
Spanish: cockroach
Swahili: safari
Swedish: ombudsman

Tagalog: boondocks
Tahitian: tattoo
Taino: potato
Tamil: pariah
Telugu: tomtom
Temne: cola
Thai: samlor (a three-wheeled vehicle, frequently motorized, used as a taxi)
Tibetan: polo
Tlingit: hooch
Tongan: taboo
Tswana: tsetse
Turkish: jackal
Tupi: cashew
Twi: obeah (an amulet, charm, or fetish used for magical purposes)

Ukrainian: nebbish
Urdu: coolie

Vietnamese: Tet (the Vietnamese lunar New Year)
Welsh: flannel
Wiradhuri: kookaburra (a large, arboreal, brown kingfisher)
Wolof: juke

Xhosa: quagga

Yiddish: oy

Yoruba: oba (the title of the ruler of the ancient West African kingdom of Benin)

Zulu: mamba (a large venomous African snake)

Sometimes we use words from other languages without completely assimilating them so that they retain a measure of their original orthography, pronunciation, and flavour. Some words are so closely associated with their native language that we are loath to translate them. For example, we could translate *Weltanschauung* as "world view" but it may be felt that the term loses something in the translation. Many words from French and Italian fall into this category. A few examples include "*auberge*," "*bourgeois*," and "*concierge*" from French, and "*adagio*," "*allegro*," and "*bravura*" from Italian. In many cases we keep phrases in their original language rather than attempting to translate the concepts. From Latin we have terms such as "*ad infinitum*," "*de novo*," and "*ipso facto*." And of course we use many French phrases daily: "*à la mode*," "*après ski*," "*avant-garde*," "*café au lait*," "*cul de sac*," "*enfant terrible*," "*esprit de corps*," "*haute cuisine*," "*laissez-faire*," and "*ménage à trois*." Unlike other languages where borrowings might be seen as cool but rarely as a sign of erudition, in the English-speaking world, they are seen as a sign of sophistication and worldliness. It could be argued that some of these terms are pretentious and vain and that an Anglo-Saxon term expresses the concept just as well. But language is often used not only to communicate ideas but to convey an attitude. Many English-speaking people enjoy using these foreign phraseologies because they believe they impart a certain cachet to a conversation.

Usually when a food word is absorbed into English, it retains its original pronunciation, giving the food a more exotic appeal. While the absorption of foreign words into English accelerated in the 20th century, the process started much earlier. The following chronological list highlights the various languages that have flavoured our vernacular, not to mention our diet. Because so many foods and beverages came early into English by way of the Normans, I have started the list in the 16th century. The dates indicate the first time the word appears in English, according to the *Oxford English Dictionary*.

Many words have entered English not by direct contact with the language that is their source, but indirectly through an intermediary language. Many of the earlier Italian loans came to us via French, the Italian of the Renaissance having voyaged to France before reaching the shores of England. The Italian "*battaglione*" passed into French as "*bataillon*" before reaching English as "battalion." "Musket" came to English from the French "*mousquet*," which in turn came from the Italian "*moschetto*."

Many of the earliest loan words from the East migrated via Latin, a large number having first passed through Greek. "Elephant," for example, migrated from Egyptian, through Greek, Latin, and French. "Albatross" is based on a Phoenician word which drifted successively into Greek, Arabic, and Portuguese, and then reached English.

Foreign words, when adopted into English, have always been used freely with native prefixes and suffixes. English adverbs ending in "-ly," adjectives ending in "-ful," and nouns ending in "-ness" or "-ship" are found with words of French origin almost as frequently as with words of English origin. In this domain we have adverbs such as "nicely" and "beautifully," and nouns such as "companionship" and "gentleness."

The names of some ethnic groups have tunneled their way into words via fascinating etymological journeys. The Germanic Franks (the term "France" is derived from the name of this ethnic group) have bequeathed their name to our language. In Frankish Gaul, only the Franks had the status of freemen, that is, people free of restraint or restrictions. By the middle of the 16th century, the word "frank" came to mean one who is candid and outspoken.

The name of another Germanic tribe, the Goths, has become an English word, albeit in an unwarranted manner. The Goths overthrew Rome in the 5th century and dominated much of Europe for the next three hundred years. Although they did not employ Gothic architecture with its characteristic pointed arches in their designs, Renaissance architects bestowed the term "gothic" on all buildings characteristic of the Middle Ages. The Renaissance considered them unsophisticated and crude, and hence suitable for the barbaric Goths.

At one time "Bohemian" referred to someone from Bohemia, a historic region in the western Czech Republic. The term was associated with Gypsies, in the mistaken belief that Bohemia was the port of entry for Gypsies into the West. This sense began to change after 1848 when William Thackeray described the character Becky Sharp in *Vanity Fair* as "of a wild, roving nature, inherited from father and mother, who were both Bohemians by taste and circumstance." Thenceforth the term has been used to describe artists and others with unconventional tastes.

The ancient citizens of the Greek city-state of Sparta have bequeathed not one but two adjectives to our language. Because the Spartans emphasized stern discipline, the term "Spartan" has come to refer to extreme discipline

A Chronology of Food Terms Borrowed by English from Other Languages

1513: scone (Scots)
1523: profiterole (French)
1524: marmalade (Portuguese)
1530: spinach (Persian)
1531: artichoke (Arabic)
1533: pistachio (Persian)
1539: pastry (French)
1548: carob (Persian) (fruit of an evergreen leguminous tree)
1551: apricot (Arabic)
1555: bacalao (Spanish) (dried or salted codfish)
1555: cacao (Spanish)
1555: cassava (Taino)
1555: guava (Taino) (pear-shaped tropical fruit)
1555: potato (Taino)
1555: tuna (Taino) (edible fruit of a prickly pear cactus)
1556: marzipan (Italian)
1557: caraway (Greek)
1559: nectar (Greek)
1563: bologna (Italian)
1563: banana (Mande)
1567: potage (French)
1568: fricassee (French)
1572: tomato (Nahuatl)
1573: pistachio (Latin)
1577: batata (Taino) (sweet potato)
1582: salami (Italian)
1582: molasses (Portuguese)

1582: mango (Tamil)
1585: maize (Arawak)
1588: litchi (Chinese)
1588: yam (Fulani)
1590: olla podrida (Spanish)
1591: caviar (Greek)
1591: beluga (Russian)
1591: sevruga (Russian) (species of sturgeon)
1594: cognac (French)
1598: papaya (Caribbean dialect)
1598: tea (Chinese)
1598: mangosteen (Malay) (tropical fruit with sweet juicy white segments of flesh inside a reddish-brown rind)
1598: carambola (Marathi) (golden-yellow fruit of a tropical tree)
1598: curry (Tamil)
1600: couscous (Arabic)
1603: sherbet (Persian)
1604: chocolate (Nahuatl)
1611: andouillette (French) (small French sausage)
1611: omelet (French)
1611: macaroon (Italian)
1612: persimmon (Algonquin)
1612: pilaf (Persian)
1612: tapioca (Tupi)
1613: mortadella (Italian) (type of Italian sausage)

1613: coconut (Portuguese)
1613: squid (unknown origin)
1616: nectarine (French)
1616: macaroni (Italian)
1616: mochi (Japanese) (sweet
glutinous rice)
1620: tai (Japanese) (Pacific sea
bream)
1622: brandy (Dutch)
1625: panada (Portuguese)
1625: yogurt (Turkish)
1629: morello (Italian) (type of
sour cherry)
1633: sauerkraut (German)
1643: squash (Narragansett)
1643: quahog (Narragansett)
1647: bisque (French)
1647: pumpkin (Greek)
1650: matzo (Yiddish)
1653: baklava (Turkish)
1658: chard (French)
1661: gherkin (Dutch)
1662: kedgeree (Hindi) (Indian
dish of rice, lentils, onions, and
eggs)
1662: vanilla (Latin)
1662: chili (Spanish)
1664: champagne (French)
1664: ragout (French)
1664: shallot (French)
1664: celery (Italian)
1664: capsicum (Latin)
1665: ghee (Hindi)
1669: vermicelli (Italian)
1672: cranberry (German)
1673: pasta (Italian)
1673: bummalo (Marathi) (small

fish of South Asian coasts, used,
when dried, as a relish)
1673: pimento (Spanish)
1674: salmagundi (French)
(dish of chopped meat, anchovies, eggs, onions, and
condiments)
1679: soya (Chinese)
1679: okra (Igbo)
1687: sake (Japanese)
1696: soy (Chinese)
1697: Burgundy (French)
1697: avocado (Nahuatl)
1697: grouper (Portuguese)
1698: pita (Greek)
1698: dhal (Hindi)
1699: kumquat (Chinese)
1699: broccoli (Italian)
1699: tortilla (Spanish)
1703: cashew (Tupi)
1706: ramekin (Flemish) (baked
dish of cheese with bread
crumbs or eggs)
1706: cutlet (French)
1706: meringue (French)
1706: paté (French)
1706: rissole (French) (mixture of
meats and spices, coated in
bread crumbs and fried)
1707: rambutan (Malay)
1707: cocoa (Spanish)
1711: ketchup (Chinese)
1712: pekoe (Chinese)
1714: gin (Dutch)
1715: whisky (Irish Gaelic)
1723: praline (French)
1723: salpicon (Spanish) (stuffing

(stuffing for veal, beef, or
mutton, also used as a garnish)
1725: caramel (Spanish)
1725: casserole (Provençal)
1727: katsuobushi (Japanese)
(dried skipjack tuna prepared in
hard blocks)
1727: shoyu (Japanese)
(Japanese soy sauce)
1730: cookie (Dutch)
1736: salep (Turkish)
1739: cantaloupe (Italian)
1740: hyson (Chinese)
1741: seltzer (German)
1742: hors d'oeuvre (French)
1743: celeriac (Italian)
1744: waffle (Dutch)
1747: blanquette (French)
1748: torte (German)
1751: chowder (French)
1751: succotash (Narragansett)
1755: galette (French)
(broad thin cake of bread or
pastry)
1756: pumpernickel (German)
1756: callaloo (Spanish)
1760: souchong (Chinese)
1760: saucisson (French)
1760: lasagne (Italian)
1766: Roquefort (French)
1767: madeleine (French)
1771: oregano (Spanish)
1773: mocha (Arabic)
1773: pecan (Cree)
1778: pompano (Spanish)
1779: noodle (German)
1780: nan (Persian)

1784: mulligatawny (Tamil)
1788: cocoa (Spanish)
1789: aspic (French)
1792: pot-au-feu (French)
1794: cole slaw (Dutch)
1794: aubergine (Sanskrit)
1795: pe-tsai (Chinese)
(Chinese species of cabbage)
1795: soybean (Chinese)
1796: bechamel (French)
1796: bonbon (French)
1796: charlotte (French)
1796: nori (Japanese)
(Japanese edible seaweed)
1797: crêpe (French)
1799: rutabaga (Swedish)
1801: pemmican (Cree)
1802: vodka (Russian)
1805: gumbo (Angolan)
1806: crouton (French)
1806: vermouth (Greek)
1808: kasha (Russian)
1810: chapati (Hindi)
1813: soufflé (French)
1813: kebab (Turkish)
1814: Neufchâtel (French)
1814: bêche-de-mer (Portuguese)
(large sea cucumber, a delicacy
in Japan and China)
1815: consommé (French)
1815: sambal (Malay)
1817: Limburger (Dutch)
1818: cruller (Dutch) (cake of
rich dough curled and deep
fried)
1818: schnapps (German)
1822: soubise (French)

41

1823: poi (Hawaiian)
1824: timbale (French)
1824: shchi (Russian)
  (cabbage soup)
1825: brandade (Provençal)
  (dish made from salt cod)
1826: calamari (Greek)
1826: brioche (French)
1827: nougat (French)
1827: baba (Polish)
1828: vol-au-vent (French)
1830: velouté (French)
1830: kola (unknown
  African language)
1832: langouste (Provençal)
1832: garam masala (Urdu)
1832: korma (Urdu)
1833: Riesling (German)
1835: kiwi (Maori)
1836: Edam (Dutch)
1837: anisette (French)
1841: scrod (Dutch)
1841: entrecôte (French)
1841: ravioli (Italian)
1841: sultana (Italian)
1842: absinthe (French)
1845: oolong (Chinese)
1845: boudin (French)
  (blood sausage)
1845: crème caramel (French)
1845: croustade (French)
1845: mayonnaise (French)
1845: rémoulade (French)
1845: quenelle (German)
  (seasoned ball, of which the
  chief ingredient, commonly
  meat or fish, has been

reduced to a paste)
1845: basmati (Hindi)
1845: cannelloni (Italian)
1845: ziti (Italian)
1845: alfalfa (Spanish)
1845: gazpacho (Spanish)
1846: bavaroise (French)
1846: Comice (French)
1846: flan (French)
1846: halvah (Persian)
1846: chorizo (Spanish)
1846: salsa (Spanish)
1846: kugel (Yiddish)
1847: pak-choi (Chinese)
  (Chinese species of cabbage)
1848: Brie (French)
1848: frappé (French)
1849: spaghetti (Italian)
1849: choucroute (German)
  (kind of pickled cabbage)
1849: tilapia (Greek)
1851: grissini (Italian)
  (crisp bread made in long
  slender sticks)
1852: salami (Italian)
1854: kuchen (German)
1854: schnitzel (German)
1854: pirog (Russian)
1855: lager (German)
1855: wurst (German)
1855: risotto (Italian)
1855: bouillabaisse (Provençal)
1856: pretzel (German)
1856: tamale (Spanish)
1857: skyr (Icelandic)
  (dish prepared from curdled
  milk)

1858: Muenster (French)
1861: éclair (French)
1862: moussaka (Arabic)
1865: panforte (Italian)
1865: cèpe (Latin) (edible mush-
room with a smooth brown top)
1866: goulash (Hungarian)
1868: laddu (Hindi) (Indian
sweetmeat, usually made with
flour, sugar, and shortening, that
is prepared by frying before
shaping into a ball)
1869: liverwurst (German)
1869: granita (Italian)
1871: minestrone (Italian)
1872: jambalaya (Provençal)
1873: margarine (Greek)
1875: frittata (Italian)
1876: Tabasco (Spanish)
1877: Béarnaise sauce (French)
1877: chateaubriand (French)
1877: crêpe (French)
1877: duxelles (French)
1877: escarole (French)
1877: mirepoix (French)
(mixture of sautéed diced
vegetables used in various
sauces)
1877: navarin (French) (casserole
of mutton or lamb with
vegetables)
1877: ratatouille (French)
1877: tournedos (French)
1877: frankfurter (German)
1877: chipolata (Italian)
1877: ricotta (Italian)
1877: shiitake (Japanese)

1877: flageolet (Latin)
1878: Camembert (French)
1878: fondue (French)
1878: Gorgonzola (Italian)
1880: tofu (Chinese)
1880: sashimi (Japanese)
1881: tuna (Spanish)
1884: borscht (Russian)
1884: kefir (Russian) (sour-
tasting drink made from cow's
milk fermented with certain
bacteria)
1885: Gouda (Dutch)
1885: roulade (French)
1885: haroseth (Hebrew)
(mixture of apples, nuts,
and spices, eaten at the
Passover seder)
1885: tsukemono (Japanese)
(pickled vegetables, usually
served with rice)
1885: zakuska (Russian)
(Russian hors d'oeuvre
item such as caviar sandwiches)
1885: slivovitz (Serbo-Croatian)
1887: enchilada (Spanish)
1887: cola (Temne)
1888: chop suey (Chinese)
1888: vindaloo (Portuguese)
1888: kofta (Urdu) (spiced meat-
ball in Indian and Middle
Eastern cookery)
1889: rijsttafel (Dutch)
1889: hamburger (German)
1889: sauerbraten (German)
1889: wiener (German)
1889: piki (Hopi) (cornmeal

bread baked in very thin sheets
on heated stones)
1889: blini (Russian)
1889: dolma (Turkish)
(Turkish and Greek dish in
which ingredients such as rice
and meat are wrapped in grape-
vine leaves)
1890: canapé (French)
1890: cantal (French)
1891: gnocchi (Italian)
1891: aquavit (Swedish)
1892: bombe (French)
1892: mousse (French)
1892: escargot (Provençal)
1892: paella (Catalan)
1892: farfel (Yiddish)
1892: gefullte (Yiddish)
1892: kreplach (Yiddish)
1892: tsimmes (Yiddish)
1893: strudel (German)
1893: grappa (Italian)
1893: sushi (Japanese)
1893: smorgasbord (Swedish)
1894: parfait (French)
1894: zwieback (German)
(biscuit made by baking a
small loaf, and then toasting
slices until they are dry and
crisp)
1894: lassi (Hindi) (Indian drink,
made from diluted butter milk
or yogurt)
1895: millefeuille (French)
1896: paprika (Hungarian)
1898: ouzo (Greek)
1898: kimchi (Korean) (raw

strongly-flavoured vegetable
pickle, the Korean national
dish)
1898: coulibiac (Russian) (type of
Russian fish pie)
1899: croissant (French)
1899: cereal (Latin)
1899: pappardelle (Italian)
1899: tagliatelle (Italian)
1899: zabaglione (Italian)
(dessert of egg yolks, sugar,
and Marsala wine, served either
hot or cold)

and austerity. Sparta was also called Laconia, and the Laconians were thought to be terse, undemonstrative people. Hence the word "laconic" from the Greek "*Lakónikós*," "like a Laconian," entered our language to refer to one who uses few words. The Greek island of Lesbos in the Aegean Sea off the west coast of Turkey has given us another word. In the 6th century B.C. the poetess Sappho taught the art of poetry to a coterie of young women. One of the recurrent themes in her verse is the love of one woman for another, love ranging from gentle affection to sexual passion. "Lesbian" and "lesbianism" joined the English lexicon in the 19th century.

The ancient Greeks believed that the "*sardone*" ("*herba Sardonia*" in Latin), a native poisonous plant that gave the Italian island of Sardinia its name, was so deadly that anyone who ate it would develop facial convulsions and die laughing. The Greeks called this death mask "*Sardoniós gelos*" ("Sardinian laughter"). This became the French "*rire sardonique*" and our "sardonic laughter," which is laughter characterized by cynical derision.

A word coined after the name of a country originated in a letter by writer Horace Walpole. On January 28, 1754, he wrote to his friend, the diplomat Horace Mann: "I once read a silly fairy tale called The Three Princes of Serendip [a former Arabic name for Sri Lanka] ... who were always making discoveries, by accidents ... of things which they were not in quest of." He dubbed this faculty of making happy and unexpected discoveries by accident "serendipity." The *OED* states that "although formerly rare, the word and its derivatives have had a wide currency in the 20th century." The *OED* citation from a 1955 issue of *Scientific American* says that "discovery often depends on chance, or rather what has been called 'serendipity'—the chance observation falling on a receptive eye."

Dictionaries define "vandal" as "someone who maliciously destroys property." We received this word courtesy of the Vandals, a people from along the Baltic coast who attacked Europe in the 5th century. The Vandals' reputation for wanton destruction was entrenched in Western European languages as their name came to be applied to those who deface buildings, monuments, or works of art. English began using the term "vandal" to describe such a person in the 17th century. If someone says you trace your lineage to the Vandals, I suggest you take umbrage. As far as I know, no dictionary offers this caveat in front of the definition of "vandal" or "vandalize."

The word "cologne" derives from the German city of Cologne because since 1709, the scent *eau de Cologne* had been produced there. Similarly, many textile names derive from the city where they originated. French cities have contributed several fabrics to our language. We have "tulle" (from the city of Tulle), "cretonne" (from the Normandy village Creon), "cambric" (from Cambrai), "lisle" (from Lille) and "denim" (from Nîmes).The word "jeans" is a modification of "Janne," the Old French name of the Italian city of Genoa. "Satin" was named by Arab traders "*zaitûnî*," "cloth from Zaitun," (in China, now called Chuanzhou). The province of Shantung in northeast China has given its name to a soft type of silk. The Indian cities of Madras and Calicut have bequeathed us "madras" and "calico" and the fabric "muslin" derives from Mosul, Iraq. Etymologists are fairly certain that a balaclava, a close-fitting knitted covering for the head and neck, gets its name from the Crimean village of Balaclava near Sebastopol and that "fez," a brimless felt hat, derives from the city of Fez in Morocco. The patterned fabric "damask" originates in Damascus, Syria.

We get "tuxedo" from a Native American word for "wolf." In the 18th century, the name "Ptuksit" was given to a village in southeastern New York, and over time the name was altered to "Tuxedo." Near the turn of the 20th century, young men in Tuxedo started to wear dress jackets, and the name "tuxedo" caught on to refer to the apparel.

Cities have also been prominent in giving us names of foods. In this category we have "hamburger" (from Hamburg), "frankfurter" (from Frankfurt), "wiener" (from Vienna), and "baloney" (from Bologna). France has also bequeathed us the word "lyonnaise,"—"cooked with onions"— and another onion word, "scallion," gets its name from the city of Ashkelon in Israel.

The field of transportation has also contributed some city-inspired words. The word "coach" (as in "carriage") derives from the town of Kocs in northwestern Hungary. In the 15th century an unknown carriage maker in Kocs developed a larger, more comfortable carriage than any known at the time. It was called a "*Kocsi szeker*," "wagon of Kocs," which was shortened to *kocsi*. It became the rage throughout Europe and was rendered as "*kocz*" in Polish, "*kutsche*" in German, "*koets*" in Dutch, "*cocchio*" in Italian, and "*coche*" in Portuguese, French, and English. By the 16th century, it was being spelled in English as "coach."

In 1170, Thomas à Becket was murdered at a monastery in Canterbury.

He was canonized as St. Thomas of Canterbury in 1173 and a shrine was established in his honour. The next year Henry II had himself flogged at this shrine for whatever responsibility he bore in the assassination. A few days later, Henry defeated the Scots in a battle in northern England, and his victory was attributed to his recent penitence. Consequently the martyr's fame became widespread and his shrine was thronged by pilgrims, some of whom are depicted in Chaucer's *Canterbury Tales*. Since many of these pilgrims traveled by horseback, the easy, moderate gait of their horses came to be known as the "Canterbury gallop." In the 17th century this term was shortened to "canterbury" and by the 18th century to our modern-day "canter."

A small mining town in 16th-century Bohemia called Sankt Joachim-stal gave us one of our language's most valued words. Starting in 1519, money was coined from the silver mines located in Joachimstal which translates as Joachim's Valley. The coins were called "Joachimstaler" which eventually was shortened to "*thaler.*" This was adapted into Dutch as "*daler*" and a 1553 reference in the *OED* states that "the Duke of Wellington shall have for his charges 66,000 dalers." By 1600, this word began to be spelled "dollar."

Most of the words adopted from place names are nouns, but there are some exceptions. The verb "to shanghai" refers to forcing someone into an activity and more specifically into naval service. It comes from an old expression "to ship a man to Shanghai." Sailors at one point would be drugged or kidnapped and forced into service upon a ship in need of a crew. Shanghai, being a long way from the United States and a leading Chinese shipping port, was one of the destinations of shanghaied sailors. Thus the verb "to shanghai" emerged in the United States in the 1870s.

4

Early Influences

[Greek]

In my column on language in the *Montreal Gazette* of some years ago I had a series of articles crediting a variety of languages including Arabic, Chinese, French, German, Italian, and Spanish for their contributions to our vast English vocabulary. Notably absent from the listing was Greek. I received this e-mail from a reader named Dr. George Karellis:

> Every **glossologist** knows that it is neither **logical** nor **orthodox** but also an error of **colossal** dimensions to overlook the contributions of the Greek language to the **lexicon** of the English and all languages of the western world for that matter. Please note that one letter of the French **alphabet** is Greek: the **Y (I-Grec)** and the Germans use the word Zentrum (with Z to look more German) which comes from the Greek **Kentron** and many more. To verify the above you can **phone** a **scholar** in **Philadelph**ia (city of brotherly love) from the Greek "*filos*" ("friend") and "*adelfos*" ("brother") but be sure not to be a **pseudo**-scientist. This person if he (she) is free from **encephalitis, cephalalgia, glossodynia, pleurodymia,** or **proctalgia** will inform you that I am right. The suffering parts of the latter two conditions are remotely situated from the center but if severe they can cause **psychological,** or **psychiatric anomalies** and even **crises** of **neurosis** or **panic** attacks.

The sane person will inform you that **democracy** comes from the Greek as well as **astronomy, geometry, chemistry, physics, philosophy, drama, tragedy, comedy, theatre,** etc.

Needless to say the words in bold come from Greek. And in some ways, we can say, "It's all Greek to us." Many words that English absorbed from Latin were adopted originally by the Romans from Greek. The sphere of religion exhibits this pattern. English absorbed "presbyter" from Latin, which took it from the Greek "*prysbúteros*"; the Latin "*biscop*" came from the Greek "*episcopos*"; our word "monk" comes from the Latin "*munuc*," which originated from the Greek "*monachos.*"

The "dilemma"—from Greek "*dis*" ("twice") and "*lemma*" ("proposition")—in writing on Greek contributions to our language is that they are so numerous that one hardly knows where to begin. In addition to the disciplines that the good Dr. Karellis points out, the names for many others, such as biology, physics, anthropology, philosophy, psychology, and astronomy, also come from Greek. The Greek element in the English lexicon forms the core of our erudite vocabulary and dominates the technical vocabulary of technology, science, mathematics, and medicine. Entering the word "Greek" or the abbreviation "Gr" in the etymology section of the on-line *OED* yields 19,454 words of Greek origin. Some, such as *"acronym"* and *"chlorine,"* come directly from Greek without intermediary languages.

Greek has provided some of our most prolific prefixes and suffixes. If we focus only on compound words (words comprised of two or more words), where all the elements are of Greek origin, we come to comprehend the elements that are present in many words.

Take a compound word like "acrophobia." Discerning the meaning is merely a function of knowing what the individual parts mean. "Acro" denotes "height" and "phobia" means "fear," so "acrophobia" is the "fear of heights." An "acrobat" etymologically "climbs to the highest point" and the Acropolis in Athens is named using the term that means "high city." In the "phobia" family of words we also have "hydrophobia," the "dread of water," "arachnophobia," the "fear of spiders" and "agoraphobia," which means "fear of open places," since agora references a place of assembly.

Another prolific source of words we get from Greek is the "-ology" family. The suffix "-ology" denotes "the study or science of." Hence, "ontology" is the "study of being," "ideology" is the "study of ideas," "psychology" is the "study of the soul or mind," and "theology" is the "science of the divine." The "philo" affix refers to "the love of" some pursuit. This has provided us with prefixed words such as "philosophy," which is the "love of knowledge," "philanthropist" ("lover of humankind") and with suffixed words such as "necrophilia" ("lover of dead bodies") and "hemophilia" ("lover of blood," and by extension a disease in which the blood flows too freely).

The suffix "-graph/-graphy" comes from Greek and refers to what is written. In this family we have "photograph," which "writes light," "micrograph," which "writes small objects," and "calligraphy" ("beautiful writing"). "Telegraph" combines "-graph" with "tele" ("distant"), and thus means "writes from afar." The prefix "tele-" can be found in such words as "telephone" and "television." The prefix "photo" is also seen is such words as "photosynthesis" ("synthesis of light") and "photogenic" ("produced by light," and by extension "attractive in photographs").

Forms of government are well represented in Greek. With the suffix "-ocracy," which means "rule," we get "democracy" (the "rule of the people"), "aristocracy" ("rule of the best"), "theocracy" ("rule of god"), "plutocracy" ("rule of wealth"), and "autocracy" ("sole rule"). Greek has also provided us with over a hundred "-mania" words including "kleptomania" ("compulsion to steal") and "flaggellomania" ("an enthusiasm for flogging").

Greek has been a generous donor in the field of medicine. The suffix "-itis" denotes "inflammation." This has brought us scores of medical conditions, including "arthritis" ("inflammation of joints"), "laryngitis" ("inflammation of the lining membranes of the larynx"), "rhinitis" ("inflammation of the nose"), "gastritis" ("inflammation of the coatings of the stomach"), and "phlebitis" ("inflammation of the walls of a vein"). The suffix "-rhea" means "flowing" and this has brought us the lovely tandem of "diarrhea" and "gonorrhea," "*gonos*" being the Greek word for "seed." Other "Greek" diseases include "diabetes," from "*dia*" ("through") and "*bainein*" ("to go"), "leukemia," "melanoma," "emphysema," "epilepsy," and "herpes."

If I do have a gripe against Greek contributions to English, it is because some years ago I had the dubious distinction of being afflicted by a word with three Greek elements—"osteomyelitis." This refers to the "inflammation of the marrow of the bone."

Another prolific source of Greek words is the field of mythology. Lexicographer Adrian Room commented, "Many of the most familiar names of classical mythology have long been firmly rooted in our literary consciousness, where they usually rank on a popular par with Biblical figures and the more memorable characters in Shakespeare's plays." He adds, "We have all heard how Theseus killed the Minotaur ... and how Actaeon saw Diana bathing naked and was set upon by his hounds for such gross impropriety." Well, not anymore. One wonders if Sigmund Freud were formulating his theories today, whether the name of the famed Oedipus complex might not be replaced by an onanistic imperative.

The ancient myths, however, live on through the vehicle of eponyms, personal names from which words are derived. The English language is graced with several eponymous words that bear tribute to the protagonists of mythology. Many of the Greek gods bequeathed words to our language. "Dionysian" refers to drunken revelry and pays homage to the Greek god Dionysius. The Greek word for sexual love is "*eros*" and hence the Greeks dubbed their god of love "Eros." Eros bequeathed the word "erotic" to our language. From the goddess of love and beauty, Aphrodite, we have extracted "aphrodisiac"; Apollo, the god of the sun has bequeathed "apollonian" ("balanced in character") and from the primeval deity Chaos we have "chaos."

An "odyssey" is a series of long travels and pays tribute to the adventures of Homer's hero Odysseus. Homer, in *The Iliad*, presented the herald Stentor who faced the enemy and announced terms in "a voice of bronze ... as loud as fifty men together." "Stentorian" has come to mean extremely loud.

Many of the eponymous characters from Greek mythology bear witness to the vengeful and capricious nature of the gods. The nymph Echo was the quintessential gossipmonger of Greek lore. To punish her incessant nattering, Zeus and his wife Hera deprived her of all speech except the ability to echo the words of others. "Promethean" means "boldly creative" and its progenitor is Prometheus who stole fire from the gods and gave it to humanity. His eternal punishment was to be chained to a rock and have an eagle eat his liver, which would grow in the night only to be eaten again. A "Sisyphean" action is one that involves endless and futile labour. It honours Sisyphus, an ancient king of Corinth, who was sent to Hades for crimes against his subjects and condemned to forever roll a huge stone up a hill only to have gravity constantly pull it down. The word "tantalizing," meaning "tempting," doesn't hint at the agonizing torment of the hero Tantalus, the son of Zeus, who made the mistake of divulging the secret of the gods to humanity. For this defiance of the Olympian code of *omertà*, he was plunged into a pool of water in Hades, with a fruit tree just above his head. Whenever he tried to drink the water or eat the fruit they moved away from him causing him unbearable thirst and hunger.

The word "halcyon" is ostensibly a pleasant word and doesn't suggest a connection to a tragedy. It is generally defined by as "pleasingly calm or peaceful." The expression "halcyon days" refers to times of happiness and prosperity. Yet behind the calm there rages a storm. After a tempest had killed the husband of the wind goddess Alcyone, the bereft widow-goddess drowned herself in the sea. Punishing this suicide, the vengeful gods turned Alcyone and her husband Ceyx into birds, later known as "halcyons," or kingfishers, as we call them today. Alcyone's "god-father" took pity on the couple and decreed that during the halcyon's mating season, the seven days before and after the shortest day of the year, the sea would be perfectly calm. This legend continued in the Roman era, when Alcyone became Halcyone and endured well into the 15th century.

Names of birds are not the only life form derived from mythological tales. The original "python" was eponymous. According to *Brewer's Dictionary of Phrase & Fable*, "He was hatched from the mud of Deucalion's deluge, and slain by Apollo at Delphi." Even flowers enjoy mythological roots. Apollo accidentally killed the handsome Spartan lad Hyacinthus. He couldn't resuscitate him, so to assuage his guilt he made a new flower spring from the red earth and called it a "hyacinth." The flower narcissus was also born out of a death. The nymph Echo was unable to make the beautiful youth Narcissus fall in love with her, so she made him fall in love with himself and he drowned while admiring his image in a still pool. After his death, the gods changed his body into a beautiful flower, the "narcissus."

[Latin]

Although English is a Germanic language, most English speakers feel a greater affinity with the Romance languages than they do with German. Our romance with the daughters of Latin started almost fifteen hundred years ago with the mother.

In 597 A.D., the Roman missionary Augustine landed in the kingdom of Kent and brought the word of God to the heathen English. He also brought Latin words, many of which were absorbed into Old English. The Anglo-Saxons had encountered Latin before, in Europe, where several Latin words entered the language, such as "*stræt*," ("street"), "*win*" ("wine"), and "*weall*" ("wall"). They brought two or three dozen of these words with them to Britain. By contrast, the missionary influence resulted in well over four hundred new words coming into the language.

As would be expected, many of these words concerned church matters. The Old English "*préost*" ("priest") derives from the Latin "*presbyter*"; "*nunne*" ("nun") comes from the Latin term "*nonna*"; "*deacon*" ("deacon") is from "*diconus*"; "*papa*" ("pope") from "*ppa*"; "*mæsse*" ("mass") from "*messa*," and "*engel*" ("angel") from "*angelus*." The words "apostle" and "epistle" were adopted into English via the Scriptures from Greek, and "Sabbath" and "abbot" were adopted from Hebrew. At the same time, certain Old English words such as "*hefen*" ("heaven"), "*h'l*" ("hell"), and "*gód spel*" ("gospel") became imbued with a Christian connotation. Augustine and his friars brought more than words for the soul; they also brought words for the stomach. New words included "*fic*," which became "fig," "*pere*," which became "pear," "*gingifer*," which became "ginger," "*fenol*," which became "fennel," and "*m'rscmealwe*," which became "marshmallow." Improvements in agricultural techniques were reflected in the "*mattuc*" ("mattock," a digging tool) and the "*sicol*," which has become "sickle." The most important innovation was the "*mylen*," ("water mill"), a major technological breakthrough that generated more power than hitching your ox to a plow.

Other new words included "*ancor*" ("anchor") from the Latin "*ancora*," "*cycene*" ("kitchen") from "*cucîna*," "*oister*" ("oyster") from "*ostrea*," "*candel*" ("candle") from "*candela*"; "*socc*" ("sock") from "*soccus*," and "cancer," which kept the same form.

In later years many Latin words filtered into English from Latin's daughter languages, especially French. But particularly in the 16th century, we see many words coming into English directly from Latin without any spelling change: "acumen," "alias," "cadaver," "caveat," "circus," "cornea," "fungus," "hiatus," "ignoramus," "innuendo," "integer," "interim," "militia," "pollen," "radius," "sinus," "stratum," "terminus," "vacuum," "vertigo," and "virus," to give some examples. In the case of "ignoramus" and "innuendo," verb forms have been turned into nouns. In Latin "ignoramus" means "we do not know" and "innuendo" means "by nodding at."

If you asked an early 16th-century English writer why English had not produced any masterpieces for over a century, you probably would be told that it was because it possessed an impoverished vocabulary. By the end of the century, this dearth of vocabulary evaporated, largely because of the brilliance of one man, William Shakespeare. If English lacked a word that could enhance his writing, Shakespeare invented it, invariably with a Latin root. N.F. Blake points out in *Shakespeare's Language* that "Latinate words being polysyllabic, are often rhythmical and mellifluous and Shakespeare used them for that reason. ... He was always quite prepared to accept the interplay of rhythm provided by words of Latin and those of Anglo-Saxon origin." Words fashioned in this manner by the Bard include "amazement" (*Troilus and Cressida*); "castigate" (*Timon of Athens*); "frugal" (*Merry Wives of Windsor*); "hostile" (*Richard III*); "ill-tempered" (*Julius Caesar*); "lackluster" (*As You Like It*); "negotiate" and "unmitigated" (*Much Ado About Nothing*); "uncomfortable" (*Romeo and Juliet*); "uneducated" (*Love's Labour's Lost*); "useful" (*King John*); and "useless" (*The Rape of Lucrece*). Although estimates of the number of word coinages by Shakespeare vary, most observers feel that the Bard added at least fifteen hundred words to our vocabulary. He was partially able to do this by grafting Anglo-Saxon prefixes and suffixes onto Latinate words. "Premeditated" was first used in *A Midsummer Night's Dream*; Shakespeare employed the same process in creating "countless," "courtship," "paternal," and "savagery," and many other terms.

Notwithstanding that many have long considered Latin to be a dead language, English has continued to absorb words directly from Latin even in the 20th and 21st centuries. Observe "radium" (1899), "insulin" (1909), "id" (1917), "quantize" (1922), "audio" (1934), "plutonium" (1942), "video" (1958), "circadian" (1959), "condominium" (1962), "pro bono" (1969), and the latest entry, "norovirus" (2002).

[Viking Invasion]

In the *Anglo-Saxon Chronicle* under the year 787 A.D. we read, "In this year King Beorhtric married Eadburg, the daughter of Offa. And in his days there first came three ships of the Northmen from Hereáaland. ... These were the first Danish ships that came to England." So began a period of plunder of England by Scandinavian marauders that was to last over two hundred years. These invaders, however, did leave something of value behind—elements of their languages.

Before the Scandinavian invasions, Old English, like most European languages at that time, was highly inflected. Common words such as "stone" or "king" depended on word-endings to provide a meaning for which we now rely on prepositions such as "from," "to," and "with." The King in Old English was rendered as "*se cyning*" and "to the king" was "*thaem cyninge.*" Counting more than one stone in Old English entailed a change from "*stn*" ("stone") to "*stna*" ("stones"). Gradually under Scandinavian influence English became simplified and the language dispensed with complex word-endings.

The fusion of English and Scandinavian might have led to a hybrid "Scanglish" tongue, but this did not happen and English eventually prevailed. One reason was that there were far more English than Scandinavian speakers. Also, the Scandinavians, unlike the English, could neither read nor write. As a result, the Viking marauders lost their native tongues within two centuries.

The Scandinavians' languages resembled that of the Angles and the Saxons in many ways, so the incorporation of many Scandinavian elements into English was seamlessly effected without the slightest violation of the structure or the sound-system of the recipient language.

This is why we hardly consider many of the early Scandinavian borrowings into English as truly foreign. Here are some of the new words of Scandinavian lineage that came into English between the 10th and 12th centuries: "call," "crooked," "fellow," "haven," "hit," "husband," "husting," "knife," "law," "root," "sale," "score," "snare," "skin," "take," and "wrong." In some cases the original meanings of the words differed from the sense we have today. "Fellow" comes from the Old Norse "félage" which in turn derives from "leggja" ("to lay"). So the first sense of "fellow" in English was "one who lays down money in a joint venture with others." Husband comes from the Old Norse "húsbonda," with "hús" meaning "house" and "bóndi" referring to a "peasant who owned his own house and land." So the original sense of "husband" was as "master of the house." It only came to refer to a "man joined in marriage" at the end of the 13th century.

The pronouns "they," "their," and "them" were also early Scandinavian borrowings that superseded the Old English terms "hie," "hiera," and "him." Before the 12th century there was no distinctive pronoun for a female and probably as a result of Scandinavian pronunciation, the word "she" developed out of the word for "they." Probably, the most remarkable invasion of all was when the invading language took over a form of the most common English verb, the verb "to be," as its verb form "are" is of Scandinavian origin.

Many Old English terms were gradually replaced by Scandinavian upstarts such as "swelt" and "steorfan," which were replaced by "die," "wolcen" and "heofan" by "sky," "wyrt" by "root," "werp" by "cast," "hales" by "neck," "eyethirl" by "window," and "oe" replaced by "law."

Sometimes the Old English term has remained along with the word we absorbed from Scandinavian languages. In the following list of doublets, the former is of Old English origin; the latter Scandinavian:

Synonyms of Old English and Scandinavian Origin

Old English	Scandinavian
craft	skill
sick	ill
rear	raise
shatter	scatter
carve	cut
wish	want
hide	skin

It is interesting that French did not contribute many place-names in the British Isles. This probably reflects the negligible impression made by the French language on the vernacular of the English peasantry. Scandinavian names, on the other hand, are extremely common in England. There are over fifteen hundred place-names of Scandinavian origin in England, especially in Yorkshire and Lincolnshire. Over six hundred places end in "-by," the Danish word for "town" or "farm," e.g., Whitby, Rugby, and Derby. The legacy is also seen in our word "by-law." Some three hundred British place-names bear the "-thorpe" ending, such as "Althorpe" and "Ravens-thorpe." "*Thorp*" is a Scandinavian word for "village." Another common Scandinavian ending for places is "*thwaite*" ("an isolated piece of land"), as in Braithwaite.

The word "riding" for an electoral district will be familiar to Canadians and Britons. Originally, the word referred specifically to the division of Yorkshire into three administrative districts (the East, West, and North Ridings). This is because "riding" comes from the Old Norse "*priöjungr*" ("third part") from "*priöi*" ("third").

Scandinavians seem to have lost their bellicosity and have not invaded any English-speaking country in the last millennium, so the influx of words of Scandinavian origin has dried to a trickle. There have, however, been some more recent borrowings. The word "rug" came into our language in the 16th century from the Norwegian "*rugga;*" "fiord" was a 17th-century Norwegian addition, and "saga" was an 18th-century neologism that came via Old Norse and Icelandic. The word "ski" comes from the Old Norse "*skio*" ("snow-shoe, billet of cleft wood"). The first *OED* cites its first appearance in print, in 1755 in *Monthly Review*: "He says they have skies, or long and thin pieces of board, so smooth, that the peasants wade through the snow with them."

More recent additions include the Swedish "smorgasbord," a compound of "*smörgas*" ("slice of bread and butter") and "*bord*" ("board") that entered English in 1893; "ombudsman," which came in 1911 from the Swedish word "*ombud*" which means "commissioner" or "agent," and the word "slalom" that comes from the Norwegian "*slalam*" with "*sla*" meaning "sloping" and "*lam*" meaning "track."

[The Semitic Connection]

In the "so what?" category, the following headline graced the front page of a newspaper some years ago: "DNA Ties Arabs to Jews—Mideast Rivals Have Common Ancestors." The commonality is reflected not only genetically, but also in words that have meandered into English, such as the Arabic and Hebrew greeting words "*shalom*" and "*salaam*." The *OED* shows an etymological connection between the Arabic "*Allah*" and the Hebrew "*Eloah*" or "*Elohim*." The word "camel" is listed as descending from the Hebrew and Phoenician "*gamal*" and the closely associated Arabic "*jamala*." The term for an Islamic school, "*madrassa*," is connected etymologically to the body of rabbinical teachings known as "Midrash" because the Semitic root "*drs*" means something like "learn" or "receive knowledge."

The *OED* uncovers close to five hundred words with Hebrew connections but this pales in comparison to the thousand or so English words that derive from Arabic. There are many words that one would expect to be of Arabic origin such as "harem," "mosque," "sheik," and "hashish," but other entries are more surprising. The word "magazine" ultimately derives from the Arabic plural of "*makhazan*," "storehouse." The word was rendered in Spanish as "*almagagen*" and entered English via the French "*magasin*" and Italian "*magazzino*." Its first sense in the *OED* is "a place where goods are laid up; a storehouse for goods." Its usage to refer to a periodical only emerges in 1731.

The word for "the" in Arabic is "*al*," and many English words that begin with the letters "al" reflect an Arabic heritage. The word "algebra" derives from the Arabic "*al-jebr*," which means "the reuniting of broken parts." When algebra first entered the English language, it referred to the setting of broken bones, and sometimes to the fractures themselves. A faithful Arabic rendering of what we call "algebra" yields "*ilm al-jebr wa'l muqabalah*," which means "reduction and comparison by equations." The word "alcohol" comes from the Arabic "*al-koh'l*," which literally means "the kohl," the powdered antimony used as a cosmetic for darkening the eyelids. This was borrowed via French or Latin and came into 16th-century English as "*alcool*," a name for any fine powder or extract. Thus "alcool of wine" was for drinking. It wasn't until the 19th century that "alcohol" was used to refer to drinking. "Alchemy" blends the Arabic "*al*" with "*kimia*," this word coming from "*Khem*," which referenced the native name of Egypt. Alchemy was designated by the ancients as the "Egyptian art." "Alfalfa" comes from the Arabic "*alfaçfaçah*" and literally means "the best sort of fodder." "Algorithm" comes from the Arabic "*al-Khowarazmi*" which refers to a native of Khwrazm. It was also the surname of the Arab mathematician Abu Ja'far Mohammed Ben Musa, who flourished early in the 9th century; it was through the translation of his work on algebra that the Arabic numerals became generally known in Europe. "Alcove" comes from the Arabic "*al-qobbah*" ("a vault").

Sometimes we find the "al" at the end of the word, as in the word "admiral." Etymologically, the word doesn't refer to the sea; it derives from the Arabic "*amir*" ("commander") from which English also acquired the word "emir." Thus a commander of the sea is "*amir-al-bahr*"; a commander of the faithful is rendered as "*amir-al-muminin.*"

Many Arabic loan-words have enjoyed exotic etymological journeys on their way to our language. This is highlighted in food words. "Sugar" ultimately derives from the Sanskrit "*sharkara*"; it turned into Arabic "*sukkar*," which gave rise to Latin "*succarum*," Italian "*zucchero*," and Old French "*sukere.*" As mentioned earlier, "orange" traveled through Sanskrit "*naranga*," Persian "*narang*" and Arabic "*naranj*" to Spain, then French "*orange*," which was eventually rendered as "orange." The spelling without the initial "n" may have been influenced by the town of Orange in southeastern France that used to be a centre of the orange trade. Candy is also a word of ancient lineage being rendered as "*khanda*" in Sanskrit, "*qand*," in Persian and "*qandah*" in Arabic.

I had assumed that "sherbet" was a corruption of the French "*sorbet*." Not so. Terms similar to the word "sherbet" exist in Turkish, Persian, and Arabic where it is rendered as "*shariba,*" from the verb "*shariba,*" "to drink." "Aubergine" went through this transformation: "*vatinganah*" (Sanskrit), "*badingan*" (Persian), "*al-badinjan*" (Arabic), "*beringela*" (Portuguese), "*alberginia*" (Catalan), and "*aubergine*" (French).

One of the most colourful words of Arabic origin is "assassin," which literally means "hashish-eater." It entered our lexicon in 1237. The *OED* defines it thus: "Certain Muslim fanatics, in the time of the Crusades, who were sent forth by their sheik, 'the old man of the mountain,' to murder Christian leaders." These executions were committed under the influence of hashish. In virtually all European languages a word like "assassin" in French or "*asesino*" in Spanish came to be applied to one who murders for political and religious rather than personal motives.

Probably more important among the technical words that English has borrowed from Arabic is a word that forms the basis of modern mathematics, "zero." A 1940 *OED* citation from Eric Temple Bell says that "the introduction of zero as a symbol denoting the absence of units of certain powers of ten has been rated as one of the greatest practical inventions of all time." "Zero" ultimately descends from the Arabic "*çifr*" from which we also get the word "cipher." Its first citation to denote the number 0 in English occurs in 1604. Edward Grimstone's *D'Acosta Historical Indies* states: "They accompted their weekes by thirteene dayes, marking the dayes with a zero or cipher."

The terrorist attacks of September 11, 2001, and their aftermath served to popularize many Arabic words which generally are not properly understood.

Jihad: The *OED* defines "jihad" as "a religious war of Muslims against unbelievers in Islam, inculcated as a duty by the Koran and traditions." "Jihad" comes from the Arabic "jihâd," meaning struggle, contest, specifically for the propagation of Islam, although in Arabic the word is more nuanced. After a successful military campaign, the Prophet Muhammad declared that he had returned from a "lesser jihad" to a "greater jihad." When asked by a follower the nature of "greater jihad," Muhammad replied, "It is the jihad against one's soul," thereby distinguishing between the greater quest of purifying the soul of defects to become more righteous and the lesser pursuit of fighting those who subjugate Muslims. Militant Islamists have perverted the meaning of "jihad" by giving "lesser jihad" the same value as "greater jihad."

Mujahedin: The *OED* defines this word as "In Islamic countries: freedom fighters; now specifically (a body of) fundamentalist Muslims who use guerilla warfare to assert their claims." The mujahedin based in Iran and Pakistan fought the holy war (jihad) against the Soviet forces occupying Afghanistan in the late 1970s and the 1980s. The word comes from the Persian or Arabic "*mujahidin*," the plural of "*mujahid*," "one who fights in a jihad" or "holy warrior."

Fatwa: This word refers to a formal legal opinion or religious decree issued by an Islamic leader. It derives from the Arabic "*afta*" ("to decide a point of law"). The word became popularized in 1989 when the Iranian leader Ayatollah Khomeini issued a fatwa condemning novelist Salman Rushdie to death for alleged blasphemy against Islam in his novel *The Satanic Verses*. On February 23, 1998, Osama bin Laden ruled in a fatwa that "to kill Americans and their allies, both civil and military, is an individual duty of every Muslim who is able, in any country where this is possible."

Madrasa: Literally, in Arabic, "*madrasa*" is a "place for study" and derives from the verb meaning "to study." Some languages have borrowed this term and use it to refer to a religious school. I first encountered it in a prophetic article by Jeffrey Goldberg in the June 25, 2000 edition of *The New York Times*: "In a Pakistani school called the Haqqania madrasa, Osama bin Laden is a hero, the Taliban's leaders are famous alums and the next generation of mujahedeen is being militantly groomed." Afrasiab Khattak, chairman of the Human Rights Commission of Pakistan, says, "The madrasas indulge in brainwashing on a large scope, of the young children and those in their early teens."

Hijab: "*Hijab*" in Arabic means "screen." The Koran admonishes the wives of the Prophet to be behind a screen or partition in the house in the presence of visitors. This was later extended to refer to the covering of women, as well as the coverings and their veils. Usually, the "hijab" is a cloth worn over a woman's hair. The term is also applied in a general sense to mean "modest dress by Islamic women" or "Islamic covering."

Burqa: This word ultimately derives from the Arabic *"burqa,"* "to hide" or "to cover." The *OED* defines a "burka" as a garment worn in public places by Muslim women to screen them from the view of men and strangers. The first *OED* citation, from 1836, states that "the *boor'cko',* or face-veil, is a long strip of white muslin, concealing the whole of the face except the eyes, and reaching nearly to the feet." In 1884, Rudyard Kipling in *Plain Tales from the Hills* wrote, " He went ... clad in a boorka, which cloaks a man as well as a woman."

Intifada(h): "Intifada(h)" was added to the *OED* only in 1993. It refers to the Palestinian uprising in the West Bank and Gaza Strip that started in 1987. This word comes from the Arabic *"intifada,"* "a shaking off."

Although the Hebrew Bible has had a deep influence on Western culture, there are not an inordinate number of English words of Hebrew derivation. Ironically, you're as likely to hear these words voiced at a church service as anywhere else. "Armageddon" is a place-name recorded only in the New Testament's Book of Revelations: "And he gathered them together into a place called in the Hebrew tongue Armageddon." This is the location where the kings of the earth will assemble to fight against God. Armageddon is believed to be a Greek transliteration of the Hebrew phrase *"har Megiddo"* ("the mountain of Megiddo") which is near Samaria in Israel.

Hosanna: This is a transliteration of the Hebrew *"hoshia na,"* which is an imperative meaning "Save!" It is used in the Psalms, but is employed more often in the Gospels in the narrative of the entry of Jesus into Jerusalem. In its Greek form, it became part of the Christian liturgy and it continues to be used in the *Sanctus* and *Benedictus* of the Roman and other rites. "Hallelujah" translates as "Praise ye the Lord," indicating that the verb is in the plural. The command to praise is thus addressed to the members of the worshipping community. In the Hebrew Bible it is found in the Psalms; in Revelations, it introduces several hymns of praise of God. Christian liturgical usage also employs the form "alleluia" following the Greek and Latin transliterations of the Hebrew word.

Amen: This Hebrew word means "certainty" or "truth." In the Hebrew Bible it is often used as a response to someone else's statement or as a response to God's word. In the New Testament it appears not as a closing statement but as an opening affirmation of the validity of what is to follow. Thus in Matthew 5.18, we have "Amen, (for verily) I say unto you" and in John 1.51 this is doubled as "Amen, Amen, (verily, verily), I say unto you."

Satan: According to the *OED*, in the Hebrew Bible the word "Satan" "ordinarily denotes a human adversary but in some later portions (Job, Chronicles, and Zechariah), it occurs as a designation of an angelic being, who tempts men to evil and accuses them to God." The name may derive from the Semitic root "*stn*" and the most common interpretation of its meaning is "to be remote" or "to obstruct." *The Oxford Companion to the Bible (OCB)* states that although the New Testament shares many ideas about demonology with the Hebrew Bible, it is "more responsible for standardizing 'Satan' as the name for the archenemy of God in Western culture." "Satan" is rendered in many New Testament forms as "Beelzebub" ("the prince of demons") and "Baal-zebub" ("the tempter") in Matthew; "Beliar" (the evil one) in 2 Corinthians, and "Apollyon" in Revelations. "Lucifer" is a name for Satan popularized in the Middle Ages. It derives from the "merging of the New Testament tradition of the fall of Satan from heaven with an originally separate biblical tradition concerning the Morning Star." The word "devil" came into the English language in the 8th century via the Latin "*diabolus*" and the Greek "*diabolos*" ("slanderer").

Messiah: The word "Messiah" derives from the Hebrew word "*masaih*" ("anointed"). In the Hebrew Bible, the term is most often used to refer to kings whose investiture was marked by their anointing with oil. In the Jewish tradition the word denotes an expected saviour, and some applied the term to the revolutionary Bar Kokhba (135 A.D.) and the 17th-century mystic Shabbetai Zvi. The *OCB* states that the "tradition that the divinely appointed saviour should suffer has its roots in numerous psalms ... as well as to the traditional picture of Moses and the prophets as rejected and persecuted by the people."

Rabbi: The *OCB* says that the term "rabbi" only arose in the "first century C.E. [A.D.] for those ordained to be authoritative in their study, exposition, and practice of Jewish law." For this reason, the term "rabbi" is referenced in Matthew, Mark, and John, but not in the Hebrew Bible. It preserves its etymological meaning of "my master." John 1.38 states that "Jesus turned, and saw them following, and saith unto them, What seek ye? They said unto him, Rabbi (which is to say, being interpreted, Master,) where dwellest thou?" The *OCB* says that the "rabbi functioned as an interpreter of Torah and as a judge, most often of the claims of the poor. By the 3rd century, the rabbi was regarded as having magical powers such as the ability to communicate with the dead." Rabbis generally worked part-time at a trade and it wasn't until the 14th century that the word "rabbi" began to be used to refer to a "Jewish spiritual leader."

Dictionaries are teeming with names of Hebrew derivation for spiritual beings and people, as well as places and groups, such as Babel, Beelze-bub, Canaan, Essene, Goliath, Jezebel, Jonah, Pharisee, Pharaoh, and Philistine. Some of our words such as "sodomy," "satanic," "jeremiad" (recitation of mournful complaints), and "solomonic" (wise) are derivatives of these proper nouns.

Jubilee: Many English words can be traced to passages in the Hebrew Bible. A "jubilee" originally referred to a year of emancipation and restoration which according to Leviticus 25 was to be kept every fifty years and proclaimed by a blast of trumpets. The word derives from the Hebrew "*yobel*" a "ram" or "ram's horn" which trumpeted the event.

Shibboleth: A "shibboleth" refers to a catchword that marks one as a member of a group. Originally, in English, exclusion from the select group could prove deadly. "Shibboleth" in Hebrew seemingly had the innocuous meaning of an "ear of corn" and "stream in flood." Like "seashells on the seashore," it proved challenging for some to pronounce. Judges 12 tells us, "The Gileadites took the passages of Jordan before the Ephramites; and it was so, that when those Ephramites which were escaped said: Let me go over; that the men of Gilead said unto him, Art thou an Ephramite? If he said, Nay, then said they unto him, Say now Shobboleth: and he said Sibboleth: for he could not … pronounce it right. Then they took him, and slew him at the passages of Jordan."

Schlemiel: The word "schlemiel" is a somewhat offensive term for some-one who is bungling or unlucky. Its source may be an eponymous biblical progenitor who is highlighted in Numbers 1, Shlumiel. He is referred to in the Talmud as a prince who was killed while committing adultery. Even lower down the totem pole is a "schlimazel," who is the quintessential "born loser." It is said that a "schlemiel" is a person who is always spilling hot soup down the neck of a "schlimazel."

Behemoth: A "behemoth" is referenced in Job 40: "Behold now behemoth, which I made with thee; he eateth grass as an ox." The *OED* tells us that this word is the plural of *"b'hemah"* ("beast"). The *OCB* relates that "although frequently identified with the hippopotamus (as Leviathan is with the crocodile), not all the details of the creature's physiology fit this well-known mammal."

Another animal with ancient Hebraic lineage is the "camel," rendered in Hebrew and Phoenician as *"gamal."* Even our alphabet has a Hebrew and animal connection. The word "alpha" comes from the Hebrew *"aleph,"* which meant "ox" or "leader." The *OED* relates that it was "originally formed from the hieroglyph of an ox's head" and speculates that there may be an etymological connection between the elephant and the *"aleph."*

Many words are ascribed a Yiddish etymology when in fact the source is Hebraic. In this category we have *"meshuga"* ("mad, crazy, stupid") which comes from the Hebrew *"meshugga,"* participle of *"shagag"* ("to go astray"); "schmooze" ("chat, gossip") from the Hebrew for "rumour;" *"tsores,"* ultimately from the Hebrew *"sarah"*; and *"yichus"* from the Hebrew *"yihus"* ("pedigree"). "Maven" ("expert") derives from the Hebrew *"mevin"* ("understanding") and is recorded in the *OED* in 1965. A 1970 citation from L.M. Feinsilver's *The Taste of Yiddish* tells us that "Canada Dry has been touting its product as 'Maven's Choice' in American Jewish weeklies." "Tochus" may have come via the Yiddish *"tokhes"* but this in turn derives from the Hebrew *"tahat"* ("beneath"). One of its citations in the *OED* is from R.L. Pike's *Mute Witness*, written in 1963: "They call this stuff Sun Bay Ting. ... I'd call it Tuchus Pink." The *OED* defines "naches" as "among Jews, a sense of pleasure and pride at the achievements of one's children." Although the first citation of the word in English dates to 1929, it wasn't until 1993 that the *OED* added this distinctive word to its ranks.

Occasionally, even the *OED* misses the Hebraic roots. "Chutzpah" ("brazen impudence, gall") is shown as deriving from Yiddish. Sixteen hundred years ago in the Talmud (commentaries on the Hebrew Bible) the term implied a kind of embarrassed approval. In the tractate Sanhedrin the following observation is made of the Gentile prophet's Balaam repeated entreaties of God: "Impudence [chutzpah], even against Heaven, is of avail." In the same tractate it is written, "Chutzpah is sovereignty without a crown."

While other languages treasure chastity, the English language tends to sleep with whoever it finds most attractive. In the 20th century, one of is most common bedmates has been Yiddish. Countless Yiddishisms, such as "bagel" and "kibbitz," now pepper the mainstream vernacular.

Still, as a Jewish person, I am sometimes amazed by the extent of these Yiddish inroads. Recently I phoned an editor, who is not Jewish, to see if he had received the controversial book I wanted to review. He told me he had and that in his opinion "It looked like a bunch of *dreck*." This statement surprised me; not because I held a contrary view of the book. No, what surprised me was the editor's knowledge of the word. Similarly, I was surprised when *Montreal Gazette* columnist Don Macpherson used the word "*tsuris*" instead of a conventional word such as "troubles." He wrote, "Perhaps [Premier] Bouchard was just trying to avoid unnecessary *tsuris* at the next meeting of the PQ national council." I recall hearing Bill Clinton, when president, referring to Treasury Secretary Robert Rubin's use of a "sort of cold *shtick* when he talks economics." Similarly, AT&T promotes buying goods on the Internet as a way to "shop, not *schlep*." In December 2003, Russ Smith in *New York Press* reported that "Kerry's freefall is so pronounced ... that even Dana Milbank, the Washington Post *nudnik* who specializes in needling President Bush on the most picayune details, has tossed Kerry overboard." In April 2005, Maureen Dowd in *The New York Times* wrote that Vice-President Cheney and his aides "shoehorned all their *meshugas* about Saddam's aluminum tubes, weapons labs and al-Qaeda links into Powell's UN speech." In an October 28, 2005 review in the *Globe & Mail* of the movie *Prime* starring Meryl Streep, Liam Lacey states that Streep plays a stereotypical Jewish mother who "*kvetches, plotzes,* gets *verklempt* and all those other Yiddish things."

Of course not every Yiddish usage rolls easily off every Gentile tongue. In an episode of his short-lived sitcom *George & Leo*, Bob Newhart called his pal a "schmuck" ("jerk"). This gaffe was topped some years ago in the Canadian Parliament when Saskatchewan Member of Parliament Lee

Morrison wanted to shed light on the unmitigated gall of Human Resources Minister Jane Stewart. He said, "You got to admire the jutsper (a mangling of "chutzpah") of the minister." When Morrison tried again and mangled it for a second time, Speaker of the House Gib Parent suggested, "I think you should get past the first line and then on with the question." Morrison finally spat out his question and to everyone's surprise, Deputy Prime Minister Herb Gray, who is Jewish, rose to answer. He announced that he had two words to describe Morrison's question—and all the Reform Party attacks on the Human Resources minister—"Gornisht and absolute narishkayt." Again the House was consumed by peals of laughter notwithstanding that hardly anyone in Parliament knew what Grey's words meant. Speaker Parent called for order and added, "I have no way of knowing whether these words are unparliamentary." If Parent had had access to the *OED* on-line, he could have ascertained that "narishkayt" means "foolishness." "Gornisht" (which has not yet graced the *OED*) means "nothingness."

Armed with the *OED*, Parent could have discovered that "dreck" is a word of German derivation, where it referred to excrement. According to Leo Rosten in *The Joys of Yiddish*, in English, the word "dreck" has a particular application to the arts; so my editor's use of the word to describe a book was bang-on. "Dreck" found its way into the *OED* in 1922. Its first citation is from James Joyce's *Ulysses*: "Farewell. Fare they well. Dreck!" Similarly, "tsuris" (rendered as "tsores") and "chutzpah" are now listed in the *OED*.

In Yiddish, "chutzpah" only has a negative meaning, that of "brazen effrontery or impudence." In English, however, "chutzpah" is a broader word, usually defined as "outrageous nerve," but this definition is invariably coupled with an explanation. Two of the favorite chutzpah examples are someone who kills both parents and pleads mercy before the judge because he is an orphan, and reporting your landlord for building-code violations when you're six months behind in the rent.

The *OED*'s citation of the first occurrence of the word in English is from London-born Israel Zangwill's 1892 *Children of the Ghetto*, and it conveys a positive sense. "The national Chutzbah (sic), which is variously translated enterprise, audacity, brazen impudence and cheek." Seventy-four years later "chutzpah" found a Canadian home when *Maclean's* magazine reported that "Dr. Shulman's most outstanding quality is chutzpah—a combination of enormous self-confidence and indifference to what other people think."

The online *OED* contains one hundred and forty-eight words of Yiddish derivation. Because it records any word that at any time has had currency in English, it includes some that are now obscure. One such word is "oof" (Yiddish for "money"), first recorded in 1882. "Oof" is short for "*oof-tish*" and ultimately descends from the German "*auf dem tische*" ("on the table"). We also have "oof-bird," which means "a source or supplier of money, the goose that lays the golden egg," "oofiness" ("wealth"), "oofless" ("without cash"), and "oofy" ("wealthy").

Also found is the word "*shoful*," meaning "counterfeit money." The *OED* says it is "primarily Yiddish and thence adopted in London slang." An 1828 citation from *Sessions' Papers of the Old Bailey* says "the twenty counterfeit shillings were found on me; the sister came to me (and) asked if I had my shoful about me." The verb "moskeneer" (from Yiddish "*mishken*," "to pawn") means "to pawn for more than it's worth" and surfaces in English in 1874. A peculiar entry is the word "yok," defined as "pejorative term for a Gentile; goy reversed with unvoicing of final consonant." The first citation is from A. Yezierska's *Children of Loneliness*: "She stands there like a yok with her eyes in the air."

Zangwill's *Children of the Ghetto* is the most prolific source of cited Yiddish words. The *OED* points out that these words are first mentioned in Zangwill's work: "*schnorrer*" ("scrounger"), "*schlemiel*" ("loser"), "*nebbich*" ("nobody"), "*shiksa*" ("Gentile woman"), "*shicker*" ("drunk"), "*schmuck*" ("jerk"; originally a taboo word meaning "penis"), "*rebbitzin*" ("rabbi's wife"), and the interjections "*nu*" and "*oy*."

Yiddish terms have found surprising homes. The term "*finnip*" to refer to a five-pound note is recorded back in 1839 in W.A. Miles' *Poverty, Mendacity and Crime*: "If he finds any finnips, he gives them to Nelson to fence." The term "*shicker*" is also listed in the *OED* as an Australian and New Zealand colloquialism. A 1970 citation from the *New Zealand Listener* says, "After midnight, Jerry got so shicker that he was quarreling with everyone."

Some of the most basic English words have a particular Yiddish sense. The *OED* mentions that as of 1903, the word "already" was considered to have been "Yiddishized" when placed "in final position to denote emphasis, exasperation, etc." "Need" receives a Yiddish sense in 1951 to imply something is unnecessary, as in the expression "Who needs it?" The word "so" ("without implication of preceding statement") is claimed as a Yiddish borrowing. Its first citation comes from Bernard Malamud in *Partisan Review* in 1950: "Miriam returned after 11:30. ... 'So, where did you go?' Freed asked pleasantly." The word "make" is one of the most prolific words, comprising fourteen pages of description in the *OED*. "Make" makes its Yiddish *OED* debut in 1950 in the sense of "to bring into operation, to use, affect, to concern oneself with." The first citation of this sense comes from John O'Hara's 1940 *Pal Joey*: "The poor man's Bing Crosby is still making with the throat here in Chicago."

Other literary lights are honoured by receiving the first citation of a word from Yiddish. In addition to "dreck," James Joyce's *Ulysses* gives us the first citation of "schlep": "She trudges, schlepps, trains, drags ... her load." Philip Roth's *Portnoy's Complaint* gives us two. We have "*shtup*" ("copulate"): "Why of course he was shtupping her"; and "*schlong*" ("penis"): "His schlong brings to mind the fire hoses coiled along the corridors at schools." Saul Bellow's *Herzog* provides us with the first citation in English for the word "*heimisch*," "homey, unpretentious": "A politician still found me good company, heimisch, and took me along to the races."

I lobbied some years ago in my language column for the inclusion of the word "nakhes" into the *OED*. Perhaps my effort wasn't futile. Although "*nakhes*" is not found in *Random House, American Heritage*, or *Webster's Third International* dictionary, it was added to the *OED* in 1992, albeit with the spelling "*naches*" and the following definition: "Among Jews, a sense of pleasure or pride at the achievements of one's children."

Surprisingly, the word "maven" (expert) did not show up in the list of 148 words of Yiddish derivation. At first I thought this was an omission because "maven" is listed in several American dictionaries. "Maven" is, however, found in the *OED* but it is listed as being derived from the Hebrew "*mevin*" ("understanding"). Similiarly, "*goy*" (Gentile) ultimately comes from Hebrew where it means "nation."

5

English is Poorly Pronounced French

The movie *Saving Private Ryan* featured some graphic scenes of the D-Day invasion by American, British, and Canadian forces onto the beaches of Normandy on June 6, 1944. The soldiers that day were somewhat preoccupied and can be forgiven for not thinking about the invasion in reverse from Normandy to Britain which occurred 878 years earlier. For this invasion was to change the English language forever.

I speak of course of the invasion of the British Isles by the Normans that took place at Hastings. Things were going reasonably well for the heavily outnumbered Anglo-Saxon forces led by King Harold, until Harold was killed by an arching arrow that pierced his right eye. Two of Harold's brothers had already fallen at the battlefield and the leaderless English army retreated, allowing the forces led by William the Conqueror to prevail on October 13, 1066. On Christmas day that year, William was crowned King of England and French then became the official language of the land. The Normans quickly took control of the instruments of power. William appointed two Normans to serve as archbishops of England. By 1072, only one of the twelve earls was an Englishman and he was executed four years later.

Things didn't change much for the English regardless of their social class. Everybody still ate, drank, and belched in English, worked and played, spoke, laughed and also sang, walked, ran, rode, leaped, and swam in English. They lived in houses with halls, rooms, windows, doors, floors, steps, roofs, and gates. The Englishman's "spirit" might be French but his mind was still English, as were his body and nearly all its parts: arm, arse, bollock, blood, brain, breast, ear, eye, finger, foot, hand, head, heart, knee, leg, lip, liver, lung, mouth, nose, throat, tongue, and tooth.

The English lived in cottages; the Normans in French *maneirs* or *castels*. The English did most of the *werc*; the Normans enjoyed most of the *leisir* and the *profit*. Life was hard for the English and the Normans had it fairly *aisé*.

French words didn't inundate the English language immediately after the Norman Invasion. The flood didn't start until the middle of the 13th century and it continued unabated for two hundred years. Between 1250 and 1400, when Chaucer died, the English language took in 43 per cent of its French loan words. For two centuries after the Invasion, French was the language of the upper classes in England. At first those who spoke French were of Norman origin, but soon, through marriage and association with the ruling class, many people of English extraction must have found it advantageous to speak French. Of course, it worked both ways. Many Norman men took English wives and had children who would be spoken to in English by the mother. Also a French soldier on a manor amidst hundreds of English-speaking peasants was bound to learn some English.

At the beginning of the 13th century, England had control of two-thirds of France. If this situation had endured, French might have remained the dominant language in England. But England was starting to lose her possessions abroad and a sense of rivalry was developing between England and France that culminated in the Hundred Years War. Language was starting to be equated with patriotism, resulting in calls for a greater status to be attached to the English language. In 1356, the mayor of London ordered that court proceedings there be transacted in English, not French. By 1362, Parliament extended this rule nationwide declaring that "French is much unknown." In 1385, Parliament was convened in English and that same year scholar John Trevisa declared that "in all the grammar schools in England, children leave French to construe and learn in English." Fifty years earlier the curriculum had been entirely in French. In 1399, when Henry IV became king, he was the first monarch since the Invasion to be more fluent in English than in French. About the same time, Oxford University introduced a statute that students be taught at least partially in French "lest the French language be entirely disused." It was a losing battle. By the 15th century, usage of French had all but disappeared in England.

But if French had disappeared, it was because it had been incorporated into English. Robert Claiborne in *Our Marvellous Native Tongue* highlights this by translating into modern English a resolution by the London Guild of Brewers in 1420 in which English is formally declared to be the official language of their meetings:

Whereas our mother tongue ... hath in modern days began to be honourably enlarged and adorned; for that our most excellent lord King Henry the Fifth hath, in his letters missive and diverse affairs touching his own person, more willingly chosen to declare the secrets of his will, and for the better understanding of his people hath, with a diligent mind, procured the common idiom ... and there are many of our craft of brewers who have the knowledge of writing and reading in the said English idiom, but others [i.e., Latin and French] ... they do not in any wise understand; for which causes ... it being considered how the greater part of the Lords and trusty Commons [i.e., Parliament] have begun to make their matters to be noted down in our mother tongue so we also in our craft, following in some manner their steps, have decreed in future to commit to memory the needful things which concern us.

As the discerning reader will have noted, many of the words in this passage had been absorbed from French within the previous two centuries. In many cases French words were grafted onto English suffixes, giving us such words as "adorned," "honourably," and "touching." Let's look at how this absorption process occurred.

I find it puzzling that organizations whose raison d'être is to "protect" the French language, such as the Office de la langue française in Quebec or L'Académie française in France, feel such urgency to avoid pernicious anglicisms and create distinct French terms. The English invasion is actually no more than a trickle. Years ago, a study was made of the French newspaper *Le Monde* and it was found that only one word in one hundred and sixty-six was English. I believe French should absorb even more English words. English has by far the largest vocabulary of all languages, more than double its nearest competitor, German. Yet, not more than one-third of English vocabulary comes from the original Anglo-Saxon word stock. Actually, sometimes it seems English is essentially poorly-pronounced French. To highlight the Gallicisms in the English language, I give you an original piece of literature entitled "A Fête Worse Than Death." All the italicized words derive from French.

It was a *fête* worse than death. The *famished invitees* included *la crème de la crème*: a *stupid duke*, a *grotesque baron*, a *naive princess*, a *lieutenant* with a handle*bar moustache*, a *gross colonel*, a *blasé grande dame*, a *coquettish brunette femme fatale* with her *risqué* yet *petit-bourgeois beau*, a *gauche, nouveau riche bon vivant* accompanied by his *avant-garde* and *svelte fiancée* and a *blonde ingenue* on the arm of a *parvenu entrepreneur blemished* as a *roué* because of his *ménage à trois* with the *au pair* and the *marquess*.

The *repast* was *horrible*. The *salad* consisted of two *puny pieces* of *lettuce garnished* with *croutons* and barrels of *oil* and *vinegar*. The *Camembert* and *brie* were *tarnished*, being *mauve* and *puce* respectively, the *soup* and *chowder* were *very* cold and the *crêpe hors d'oeuvres* were *moldy*. The *menu* was *large*. It included *bacon, sausage, filet mignon* with *béarnaise sauce, légumes, shallots, paté, poultry, salmon, sole*, and *mackerel*. For *dessert*, there was a *pastiche* of *tarts, jellies, nougat, crème caramel, éclairs*, and *sorbets*. *Fruits* included *grapes, oranges, cherries, lemons*, and *melons*. The *chef's efforts* were definitely not *haute cuisine*. Not only was the food not *delicious*, it was *odious*. Wines included *burgundy, champagne*, and *claret*; spirits were *bourbon* and *cognac*, and the *liqueurs* were comprised of *anisette, cointreau, crème de cacao, crème de menthe*, and *frappés*.

The *soirée finished abysmally* as the *entertainment* was also a *debacle*. The *chanteuse* couldn't sing, the *clairvoyant* couldn't tell the *future*, the *raconteur* couldn't tell a *story*, the *magician* was *maladroit*, and the *ballet dancer* didn't know a *plié* from a *jeté*. The *movie* was a *première* in the *cinema verité genre*, so *clichéd* that *several people* either *vanished* or *expired* of *ennui*. They were *transported* to the *morgue*.

Francophone spurners of anglicisms claim that in the 20th century the traffic has been unidirectional; words are flooding into French from English, whereas the flow of French words into English has essentially stopped. I disagree. While the Gallic word-stream may not be running as vigourously of late, it is still flowing steadily.

The first decade of the 20th century saw the adaptation of many transportation words from French. The fledgling field of aviation provided us with "fuselage," from the word "*fuseau*" ("a spondle"), a reference to its shape, and "aileron," one of the hinged flaps on the trailing edge of a wing for maintaining or restoring balance when flying. "Aileron" derives from the French word for wing, "*aile*." The word "hangar," in the sense of "an airplane shed," arrived from French in 1902. Motor vehicles bequeathed within the first three years of the century the trilogy of "chassis," "chauffeur," and "limousine." "Chassis," the base-frame of a car, comes from the French "*chassis*" ("frame"). Chauffeur actually emerged in English in the last decade of the 19th century, but it had the sense of "motorist"; an *OED* citation from 1903 states that "All the members of the Italian Royal family are enthusiastic chauffeurs," but this was soon elbowed out by the current sense. The French word is derived from "*chauffer*" ("to heat") and first designated a stoker. For "limousine," the *OED* notes that "originally, the driver's seat was outside though covered with a roof."

French has also contributed some relatively recent words in the sphere of politics. "Détente" comes into English in 1908. It is taken from the French where it literally means "loosening, relaxation." The term became particularly popular during the waning years of the Cold War when it referred to a relaxation of tension between the East and the West. The word "reparations" had been adopted into English from French in the early 15th century, but the specific 20th-century plural usage came from the French term "*reparations*" in the French text of the 1919 peace treaty, detailing payments to be made by Germany.

And would we have anywhere to dine without the French? "Restaurant" first graced our language in 1827, and was followed in 1864 by "brasserie," "charcuterie" in 1858 (Germanic "delicatessen" only arrives in 1877), and "bistro" in 1922. "Bistro" may have arrived in French a century earlier in a bizarre fashion. When the Russians invaded Paris after Napoleon I's fall in 1815, it is alleged that restaurant owners would lure Russians into their eateries by shouting the Russian word "*bee-stra*," meaning "quick," assuring them that they could eat quickly and cheaply. "*Bee-stra*" mutated into "bistro," which connotes a small unpretentious restaurant serving inexpensive meals.

When we enter a restaurant, we're liable to be greeted by a "maître d'" (short for "maître d'hôtel"), which makes its English-language debut in 1899. We might eat a "buffet," (an 1888 addition to English) and might have to choose between "haute cuisine," a 1926 addition designating classic French cooking with rich sauces, or "nouvelle cuisine," a 1975 selection which denotes a modern style of cooking emphasizing fresh, local ingredients and imaginative presentation. Although the majority of French food terms predate the 20th century, there are still some recent additions. "Coq au vin" first graces the *OED* in 1938, "cassoulet" in 1939, and "crudités" in 1960. While certain dishes such as "*boeuf bourguignon*" and "*coquilles St-Jacques*" may not be listed in the *OED*, these terms are always referenced as such and not in some anglicized form.

What makes French loan-words stand out is the long association of French with social desirability. Throughout the English-speaking world, adding a *soupçon* of French to your vocabulary is still a statement of the kind of person you are—a highbrow equivalent of the car you drive. The antipathy some francophones have towards anglicisms might be allayed if they realized how much the French heritage of English is celebrated by its speakers.

Because the Norman Conquest made French the official language of the ruling elite, many of our words having to do with government and administration come from French. The total French influence is still exemplified in virtually all the English words that relate to government, administration, or religious authority. Observe "government," "administration," "country," "court," "state," "judge," "soldier," and "sacrament" to name but a few. The French word "crime" replaced the English word "sin," which began to refer only to spiritual misdemeanors.

Two of the earliest to trickle into English are "chancellor" around 1066 and "castle" in 1075. By the 12th century more words start flowing into English. "Prison" arrives in 1123. The first *OED* citation is from the Old English Chronicles: "He let niman on prisune don." "Justice" is first recorded in 1137. The year 1154 marks the arrival of "miracle," "peace," and "market," adopted from the French "*marché*." The word "miracle" also surfaces in English in 1154, and "juggler," "fruit," "grace," "large," "manner," "passion," "sacrament," and "saint" first appear in 1175; "jury" is added in 1188.

The earlier part of the 13th century brings still more words. "Baptist," "baron," "easy," "feast," "flower," "honour," "pay," "sergeant," and "virgin" arrive in 1200 and "duke" arrives in 1205. Parliament first convenes in our language in 1216. The year 1225 highlights the first citation of many words in English such as "boil," "champion," "consent," "dame," "devout," "dignity," "doubt," "estate," "form," "gentle," "habit," "letter," "noble," "physician," "pity," "preach," "prince," "scourge," "servant," "state," and "traitor."

Between 1250 and 1400, over 40 per cent of our French borrowings came into English. "Enter" arrives in 1250, "count" in 1258, and "park" in 1260. Appearing in 1275 are "clergy," "fool," "fry," "jail," "language," "mutton," "pork," "sermon," and "service." Three years later the word "plaintiff" joins our lexicon. "Mustard" arrives in 1289, and the following year sees the addition of "conduct," "face," "felony," "grape," "herb," "homage," "palace," "pray," and "solace." "Perjury" surfaces in 1292. The words "age," "balance," "bastard," "chivalry," "country," "eager," "forest," "judgment," "manner," "marriage," "mayor," "roast," "safe," and "touch" come in 1297. "Sugar" arrives in our language in 1299 via the Old French "çucre," but the word ultimately derives from Arabic. "Beef," "Christianity," "convent," "court," "descend," "enemy," "sacrifice," "soldier," "sturgeon," and "vestment" join our vocabulary in 1300; "attorney," "horrible," and "judge" arrive in 1303; "chastity" in 1305; "defendant" in 1314; "remember" in 1330; "sober" in 1338; "chaplain," "oppression," and "temptation" in 1340; "sole" (the fish) in 1347; "broil," "lieutenant," "literature," and "question" in 1375; "captain" and "confession" in 1380; "crime" and "liberty" in 1382; "magic" in 1384; "army" and "veal" in 1386; "nurse" and "viscount" in 1387 and "carriage" in 1388. The *OED* lists a host of words such as "perch," "salmon," and "season," which arrive at some undetermined point in the 14th century.

In some cases words also took on added senses in this period. "Peace" is recorded in 1154 in the sense of freedom from civil commotion; by 1297 it also refers to the cessation of war.

If domination in a particular field is embarrassing, then I suppose English-speaking people should eat with the greatest sense of shame, for hardly a food word in our language aside from bread is of Anglo-Saxon origin. By far the largest number of words comes from, or via, French.

Observe the following all-French food list: "bacon," "beef," "cabbage," "carrot," "cauliflower," "cherry," "chowder," "crepe," "grape," "jellies," "legumes," "lemon," "lettuce," "mackerel," "melon," "mutton," "nougat," "omelet," "onion," "orange," "pheasant," "poultry," "raisin," "salad," "salmon," "sauce," "sausage," "shallot," "sole," "soup," "tart," "veal," and "venison." Even the words "fruit" and "vegetable" (notwithstanding that the word for vegetable in French is "*légume*") are French. The list of French words connected to eating is seemingly endless: "cuisine," "dessert," "diet," "dinner," "menu," "supper," and many others. Many of our cooking techniques are French, for example, "gratinée," "sauté," and "purée." Even the basics are French, such as "boil," "broil," "fry," "stew," and "roast." The original Old English cooking word, which can be found in *Beowulf*, was "seethe," which referred to boiling food. Now the heated sense as in "seething with rage" is mostly metaphorical.

Old English had a vocabulary of around fifty thousand words and was very short on adjectives. The Norman Invasion solved this descriptive impoverishment by giving us such adjectives as "abundant," "active," "brief," "calm," "chaste," "easy," "foreign," "innocent," "natural," "rude," "safe," "savage," and "tender."

Old English had a distinct lack of terms to measure quantity or refinement. This was, of course, changed thanks to French imports. In this sphere we have "abundant," "active," "amorous," "brief," "calm," "chaste," "common," "covetous," "cautious," "easy," "feeble," "foreign," "gentle," "hasty," "innocent," "jolly," "luxurious," "moist," "natural," "obedient," "pertinent," "plain," "quaint," "rude," "safe," "savage," "sudden," "tender," "treacherous," "universal," and "usual."

Only 4,500 words remain in current English from Old English, but they are fundamental English words such as "man," "wife," "child," "brother," "sister," "live," "fight," "love," "drink," "sleep," "eat," and "house" and various connectives such as "to," "for," "but," "and," "at," "in," and "on."

French livened up English by also literally bringing colour to our language, adding many shades to the English spectrum of colours. *Vive la vie en* "auburn," "beige," "carnation," "chartreuse," "écru," "jonquil," "puce," and "taupe," which have all brightened up our language.

One might argue that *The Oxford Companion to the English Language* (*OCEL*) is missing an "s" at the end of its title. It has headings for over four hundred varieties of our multitudinous mother tongues, such as Australian English, Singapore English, Indian English, and Black Vernacular English. I've never even heard of some of the varieties, such as Babu English, which is described as "a mode of address and reference in several Indo-Aryan languages, including Hindi, for officials working for rajahs, landlords, etc."

My mother tongue is actually one of these mutants listed in *OCEL*. In my dealings with the outside world, I'm constantly being reminded of the distinctiveness of my English. In fact, as a Quebec anglophone, I insist on being regarded as a member of a distinct society.

I recall many years ago having given an American telephone reception-ist my phone number and adding that "my local was 222." She ejaculated, "Your what?" I quickly corrected myself and said, "My extension is 222." Similarly, I once left a Newfoundland customer perplexed when I told him I would try to locate an item for him at one of our "filials" instead of using the word "subsidiaries."

I had just been guilty of speaking Quebec English.

It is taken for granted that English influences French in Canada. One hears terms like "*le snack bar*," "*chequer*" instead of "*verifier*," and "*untowing*" instead of "*remorque*" for a tow truck. The French of the business world includes anglicisms such as "*meeting*," "*cash flow*," "*marketing*," and "*downsize*." The prevalence of anglicisms is one of the reasons some Québécois feel that their language is being threatened.

More and more, however, the flow isn't unidirectional. Many of the following are Quebec French terms in common use in English: "métro" ("the subway"); "C.É.G.E.P." (*Collège d'Enseignement générale et professionel*"—the system of junior colleges in Quebec); "CLSC" ("*Centre Local des Services Communautaires*"—"local health and social services centre"); "classes d'accueil" ("welcoming classes"); "caisse populaire" ("cooperative bank"); "Péquiste" (member of the Parti Québécois); "pure laine" ("old stock," ethnically speaking); and "dépanneur" ("convenience store"). These are all terms that Quebec anglophones are likely to use in their original form rather than translating them into English.

One hears many usages which prove that Quebec English is a real phenomenon. As a demonstration of the distinctiveness of Quebec English, I've concocted the following, with "translations" in parentheses:

The *professor* (high school teacher) at the *polyvalent* (high school) believed that s*cholarity* (schooling) was being affected by students' *cons-ecrating* (devoting) more time to *manifestations* (student demon-strations) about the dress code than to their *notes* (grades). During his *conferences* (lectures) their inattention was hurting their *apprenticeship* (learning).

He also felt he was getting *collaboration* (cooperation) from his *confreres* (co-workers) in better serving the *collectivity* (community). He checked his *coordinates* (timetable) and set up a *rendezvous* (meeting) with the *Director-General* (principal), Monsieur Langlois, and stated that it was a *primordial* (essential) consideration that some teachers be released before they reached *permanence* (tenure) under the *syndicate* (union) agreement. Monsieur Langlois wrote back saying that he was aware of the problem and had requested a *subvention* (grant) in the *annex* (appendix) to his *planification* (policy) budget to the *confessional* (denominational) school board in order that *formation modalities* (training methods) be created to make teachers more dynamic *animators* (group leaders).

Some of these terms, like "collaboration," "rendezvous," and "annex" could be used in non-Quebec English contexts; however I suspect words such as "cooperation," "meeting," and "appendix" respectively are more likely to be employed.

In many cases, it's hard to know where English ends and French begins. Franglais includes such classics as "hot-dog steamé ["steamed"] all dressed" and a rock music review which declared that a group's appeal was to "male white trash *de vieille souche.*" "*Vielle souche,*" like "*pure laine,*" refers to "old stock" Quebecers. But the concept of language purity is mythical. The reality is that English and French have been borrowing from each other since at least 1066 when the Normans invaded England.

The English language has not been content with merely borrowing certain words from French. In some cases, we like the word so much that we have borrowed it more than once! Examples of these doublets are: "chief/chef," "carriage/garage," "catch/chase," "cattle/chattel," "warden/guardian," "regal/royal," "launch/lance," and "wage/gauge." The first of each pair is in a Norman form and the second represents a Central French form adopted after the height of Norman influence. The French word "*gentil*" has even given us three distinct English words. Originally we absorbed it as "gentle," and the words "genteel" and "jaunty" were 17th-century additions to our vocabulary.

6

Other European Connections

[Celtic]

The seeming dearth of Celtic words in English is surprising, considering that the original Brits were Celts. After the Romans left Britain in the 5th century, the country was dominated by non-aligned Celtic chiefdoms. It didn't take long for the isle's neighbours to glean that Britain was ripe for invasion without Roman protection. In poured hordes of Jutes, Angles, Saxons, and Danes, and they pushed the Celtic Britons to the periphery of Wales, Cornwall, and Cumbria.

Linguist David Crystal claims in *The English Language* that the Celtic languages of Roman Britain had hardly any influence on the language spoken by the Anglo-Saxons. Only a handful of Celtic words came into English at the time—words such as "crag," "combe," "cross," "brock" (which means "badger"), and "tor" ("peak"). Fellow linguist Thomas Pyles echoes this in *The Origins and Development of the English Language:* "Probably no more than a dozen Celtic words other than place names were adopted by the English up to the time of the Conquest." He lists "*bratt*" ("cloak"), "*cumb*" ("valley"), "*torr*" ("peak"), and "*bannuc*" ("a bit").

Other Celtic words filtered in later on. The word "bog" is a 16th-century adaptation of the Irish or Gaelic "*bogach*" ("bog"). "Bog" has the connotation of "soft" in the Celtic "*bog-luachair*" ("bulrush"). Also coming into English in the 16th century were the pair of "plaid" from the Scots Gaelic "*plaide*" and Irish "*ploid*," meaning "blanket," and "slogan" from the Gaelic "*sluagh-ghairm*" ("host-cry"). The word "galore" is a 17th-century rendering of the Irish "*go leór*" ("to sufficiency") and the term "Tory" is really an anglicized spelling of the Irish "*tóraidhe*" ("pursuer"). The *OED* highlights this origin in its first definition of "Tory:" "In the 17th century, one of the dispossessed Irish, who became outlaws, subsisting by plundering and killing the English settlers and soldiers." "Whisky" is an 18th-century variation of "whiskybae," from the Scots Gaelic "*uisgebeatha*" ("water of life").

Linguist Loreto Todd, in the journal *English Today*, articulates the view that the number of Celtic words in English is understated by the many linguists who believe that the Anglo-Saxons borrowed many Latin words but very few from the Celtic languages. According to Todd, the view that Anglo-Saxons borrowed few Celtic words is "particularly strange if we remember that few of the Germanic invaders would have brought wives to England with them. We are asked to accept that Celtic-speaking mothers passed on only Anglo-Saxon and perhaps Latin words to their children." She also points out that many Celtic words are quite similar to English words. "Three" in Irish is "*tri*," "boat" is "*bad*," and "cat" is the same in both. Therefore, these words could just as easily be from the Celtic languages as from Anglo-Saxon. The point here is that we are dealing with a common linguistic occurrence of multiple etymologies where one can't really exclude the etymological contribution of a particular language. "Barrel" may descend from the French "*baril*" but may also be of Celtic provenance from the Welsh "*baril*" and Scots Gaelic "*baraill*." "Gable" could come from the Dutch "*gaffel*," but could descend from the Irish "*gabul*" or the Welsh "*gafl*."

The *OED* highlights this by referencing over 150 possible Celtic contributions to English. Here are some examples:

Ass (the animal): This word appears to be a modified form of the Irish term "*asal.*" The *OED* hypothesizes that the Irish word comes from the Latin "*asinus,*" but the Latin may have come from the Celtic term.

Bard: A bard was one of an ancient Celtic order of minstrel poets who composed and recited verses celebrating the legendary exploits of chieftains and heroes. It is believed to be derived from the Irish and Scottish Gaelic "*bard.*"

Bat (the stick): The Irish word for "staff" was "*bat*" or "*bata.*"

Clock: The *OED* states that "clock" does not appear to derive from any Germanic language and adds that it was "known since about the 8th century in Celtic Irish *cloc*, Gaelic *clag*, Cornish *cloch*, ... (but) not found in southern Romanic languages where *campana* is the word for 'bell.'"

Liquor: The *OED* says that "the Latin root *liqu* is by some scholars thought to represent a pre-Latin root found also in Celtic."

Todd points out that the *OED* says that the word "she" is of "difficult etymology" and that in Old English the pronoun was "*hío*," "*héo*," or "*híe*" and that Norse settlers may be responsible for changing the word to "she." But Todd also states that the word "*si*" existed in Irish and was pronounced like the modern "she." Todd hypothesizes that Irish-speakers in English monastic orders may have been responsible for the change. She also believes that many Norwegians who settled in England had previously lived in Ireland. Celtic contributions to English may not be as sparse as generally supposed.

[Dutch]

Robert Hendrickson relates in *Word and Phrase Origins* that the "Dutch people have been so offended by the English language over the past three centuries that in 1934 their government decided to drop the word 'Dutch' and use 'Netherlands' whenever possible." Although not used as often in recent years, there are approximately sixty expressions in English featuring the word "Dutch" that highlight supposedly negative qualities of the Dutch. We have "Dutch courage" (bravery inspired by alcohol); "Dutch uncle" (an old busybody who reprimands young people); "Dutch defense" (surrender); "Dutch act" (suicide); and "Dutch treat" (a meal or entertainment where each pays their own way).

Hendrickson speculates that dissing the Dutch "began with the bitter hostilities between Britain and Holland in the 17th century, when the Dutch colonial empire threatened to usurp Britain's own." In any case, most of the pejorative "Dutch" expressions are no longer in vogue. The enduring legacy of Dutch to our language remains in the many words bequeathed to English.

Many of these words hearken back to the 17th-century naval rivalry between Holland and England. English absorbed the word "sloop" from the Dutch "*sloep*"; "boom" from the Dutch "*boom*" ("tree," "beam," "pole"); and "cruise" from the Dutch "*kruisen*" ("cross"). In the 16th century the Dutch began building light, speedy ships designed to chase the ships of pirates and smugglers. These vessels were called "*jaghtschips*," literally "ships for chasing," and the word "yacht" is first recorded in English in 1557. The word "smuggler" itself comes from the Dutch "*smokkelaar*" and the first *OED* citation from 1661 is more faithful to the Dutch spelling than the modern English rendition: "A sort of leud people called Smuckellors, never heard of before and late disordered times, who make it their trade … to steal and defraud His Majesty of His Customs." The word "filibuster" ultimately comes from the Dutch "*vrijbuiter*" ("freebooter"). The *OED* defines "freebooter" as "one who goes in search of plunder, especially a pirate." Filibuster retains a taste of piracy in the sense that it holds a piece of legislation captive.

A commonly smuggled item, alcoholic beverages, also exhibits a strong Dutch provenance. The word "brandy" is a shortened version of "brandy-wine," which descends from the Dutch "*brandewijn*." "*Branden*" in Dutch means "burn" and "*wijn*" means "wine." "Gin" is actually a shortened version of "geneva," which comes from the Dutch "*genever*." The *OED* relates that geneva is "a spirit … flavoured with the juice of juniper berries." But in the shortened form of "gin" the denotation is of a drink of British manufacture, which originally was an imitation of the Dutch spirit. The word "booze" is an early 14th-century addition to our vocabulary. It derives from the Dutch "*bksen*," "to drink to excess."

Dutch has not been a prolific source of food words into English. Two food contributions from Dutch, however, are "cookie" and "coleslaw." "Cookie" doesn't come from "cook," as one might expect, but from "cake," and "cake" comes into English from the Dutch "*koekje*," diminutive of "*koek*" ("cake"). "Coleslaw" derives from the Dutch "*koolsla*," a reduced form of "*kool*," "cabbage" plus "salad."

The early American colonists disliked the term "master" with its elitist allusions and were happy to import a more homey word from the Dutch. The Dutch word "*baas*" was rendered originally in English as "bass" and finally as "boss." It is noted by the *OED* as occurring as early as 1649, but it was considered too slangy for the taste of many a purist, some of whom were upstart Americans, such as novelist James Fenimore Cooper who condemned the word as a vulgarism in 1838.

Another probable Dutch Americanism is "Yankee." Many etymologists believe the term comes from "*Jan Kees*," a version of "*Jan Kaas*" ("John Cheese"). Another theory has the word deriving from the Dutch "*Janke*," a diminutive of "*Jan*" ("John"). "Yankee" was first used as a pejorative term for American colonials by the British military. In 1758, General James Wolfe used this term to express his low opinion of the American troops assigned to him. It was not until the Battle of Lexington, the first skirmish in the American Revolution in 1775, that Americans began applying the word "Yankee" to themselves and wearing the nickname with pride. A 1775 *OED* citation confirms this, with an editor's note following the citation: "Yankies—a term formerly of derision, but now merely of distinction, given to the people of the four eastern states."

No description of Dutch contributions to our language would be complete without a short history of the creation of "Santa Claus." When the Dutch came to *Nieuw Amsterdam* (later New York) in the 17th century, they brought tales of their patron saint, Saint Nikolaas. The English heard this as "Sint Klaas" or "Sinterklaas" and over time these terms mutated into Santa Claus.

To their credit, the Dutch are not a petty, mean-spirited lot. Notwithstanding the many pejorative Dutch terms that litter our language, the Dutch happily speak English as a second language and they have not retaliated with English courage, treats, or uncles.

[German]
When French gastronome Anthelme Savarin asserted, "Dis-moi ce que tu manges, je te dirai ce que tu es," he may have been claiming subliminally that anglos are essentially French, because the majority of our food words come from French. But whereas we anglo animals are etymologically French, our minerals are German. All the following are of German origin: "bismuth," "cobalt," "cyanite," "feldspar," "gneiss," "graben," "hornblende," "kainite," "kunzite," "nickel," "quartz," and "zinc." One would be hard pressed to find a rock not discovered by a German. The *OED* lists over thirty minerals from "bredigite" to "zippeite" that were named in honour of Geman mineralogists.

One wouldn't expect the field of mineralogy to be a hotbed of demons but such is the case. "Cobalt" comes from the German "*Kobold*," the name of a mountain-dwelling gnome in the lore of miners. The term "kobalt" came to be applied to cobalt-containing ores extracted by 16th-century German miners. It was a pejorative term, because the ore was considered worthless at that time. In addition, arsenic and sulfur contaminants found in the ore could cause ulcerations of the hands and feet. It was believed that cobalt ore was harmful to the neighbouring silver ore, or actually had been left behind as a kind of changeling by the mountain goblin who stole the silver.

"Nickel" was given its name by Swedish mineralogist Axel F. Von Cronstedt in 1754. But nickel had been synonymous with "*Kobold*" in some German dialects in which it meant "rascal" or "devil." Niccolite, a frequent component of cobalt ores, was known in German as "*Kupfernickel*," "copper-nickel." Just as cobalt ore was a disappointment to those seeking silver, so the copper-coloured niccolite was an unwelcome substitute for valuable copper. *Kupfernickel* may have been named as a sort of "fool's copper" by those who believed that it had been substituted by a malicious sprite.

Another "nickel" word of German origin is "pumpernickel." One folk etymology had the word deriving from the French expression "C'est du pain pour Nicol," Nicol being the name of Napoleon's favourite horse. While this story is false, the true origin of the word is no less devilish. Pumpernickel bread has been known to have a particular effect on the digestive system as reflected by the word which breaks into two parts: "*pumpern*," which means "to break wind," and "*Nickel*," a term for the devil. Hence, etymologically speaking, pumpernickel makes you "fart like the Devil."

German also has brought us many other food words, although not as many as we have taken from French. "Noodle" comes from the German "*Nudel*" and it arrived in English in 1779. The 19th century saw us add many food words from German including the group of "pretzel," "wurst," and "schnitzel" in the 1850s. "Pretzel" came from the German "*Pretzel*" or "*Bretzel*," which in turn came from the Old High German "*Brizzilla*." In medieval Latin, this word was rendered as "*Bracellus*" ("bracelet"). In medieval monasteries, pretzels were served to young scholars to evoke a sense of having one's arms crossed in prayer.

All these new German food words deserved a dining place of their own and so in 1877 the word "delicatessen" joined our lexicon. Etymologically, a delicatessen is a place where one eats (*essen*) delicacies. The year 1889 saw the addition of two food words of German vintage that honour the folks of Hamburg, Germany and Vienna, Austria. I speak, of course about "hamburger" and "wiener." The first *OED* citation for this new food is from 1889 from the seemingly space-deprived *Walla Walla (Washington) Union*: "You are asked if you will have 'porkchopbeefsteak-hamandegghamburgersteak—orliverandbacon.' " The same year we see the first citation of "wiener," in the *Gallup* (New Mexico) *Gleaner*: "We are willing to bet our unpaid debts, against a wiener-wurst that the modest local of the Democrat blushed more than the bride when he saw her in the diaphanous costume he describes."

Dog breeds offer another German germination domain in our language. The word "poodle" is first recorded in 1825 as a shortened version for the German *"Puddlehund." "Pudeln"* in German means "splash in the water," as poodles were used to hunt after fowl. Doberman pinschers were named after Ludwig Dobermann, a 19th-century German dog breeder. The word "pinscher" refers to the practice of clipping the dog's ears and is probably derived from the English "pinch." Dachshund literally means "badger dog" as the breed was originally developed in Germany to hunt badgers. Schnauzers derive their name from the German *"Schnauze"* ("snout"); "spitz" is a shortening of *"Spitzhund,"* with "spitz" meaning "pointed." The Rottweiler gets its name from the town of Rottweil in Germany and the Weimaraner was first bred in Weimar. The word "hound," of course, comes from the German *"Hund"* and it is first recorded as occurring in English in 897, preceding the word "dog" by two centuries.

Considering that English is a Germanic language, it has a general paucity of words from German. The influence of German on English transcends mere numbers. We have digested whole tongue twisters such as "blitzkrieg" ("lightning" + "war"), "zeitgeist" ("time" + "spirit"), "poltergeist"("noise" + "ghost"), and "leitmotiv" ("leading" + "motive").

In other cases, rather than borrowing the words themselves, we borrow the meaning of a word or phrase and then translate it into English. This process, called "loan translation," has given us "superman" (from *"Übermensch"*). The English term was invented by George Bernard Shaw who fashioned it from the German word coined by Friedrich Nietzsche. Other examples of this genre include "beer garden" (from *"Biergarten"*), "world view" (from *"Weltanschauung"),* "wishful thinking" (from *"Wunschdenken"*), "death-wish" (from *"Todeswunsch"*), "wonder-child" (from *"Wunderkind"*), and "loan translation" (from *"Lehnübersetzung"*).

I suspect that German inroads into English have been stronger on this side of the Atlantic because of the influence of German immigrants. Whereas "bum" in the United Kingdom refers to part of the anatomy, in North America it is most often applied to a "good-for-nothing," after the German *"Bummler"* ("loafer"). The verb "hex" was first used in North

America in 1830 because of the influence of German immigrants. It comes from the German "*Hexen*" ("to practice witchcraft"). Also because of the influence of Americans of German descent, certain usages in North America show a German influence. In British English, the verb "stem" had always meant to hinder or obstruct" as in "stem the tide." For a long time in North American English, however, we have used the verb "to stem from" ("*stammen von*") to mean "originate."

While the number of loan-words in English from German isn't huge, the two languages are linked by virtue of English being a Germanic sister language. This is seen in the similarity of common words such as the familial quartet of "*Schwester*," "*Bruder*," "*Mutter*," "*Vater*," not to mention "*Haus*" ("house"), "*Gott*" ("God"), "*Wasser*" ("water"), "*regen*" ("rain"), "*Erde*" ("earth"), "*Wind*" ("wind"), and "*Feuer*" ("fire").

[Hungarian]

"Bohunk, n. Offensive slang. Used as a disparaging term for a person from east-central Europe, especially a labourer. [Blend of Bo(hemian) and Hung(arian).] Now, if 'Bohemian' actually comes from Czech, and 'Hungarian' comes from Hungarian, then 'Bohunk' comes from both."

Upon reading this comment at the newsgroup alt.usage.english, it struck me that aside from slighting Bohemians the above posting may cause blue-blooded Hungarians to take umbrage. After all, the word "Hungary" is not Hungarian. "*Magyar*" denotes a Hungarian and the country of Hungary is rendered in Hungarian as "*Magyrország*," as "*ország*" means "country."

So how did we land up with Hungary?

Actually, this question should be extended to, how did the Hungarians get to Hungary? The name "Hungary" comes from the Turkish "*Onogur*"— "*on*" meaning "ten" and "*ogur*," "arrow or tribe"—the name of a Turkish confederation of tribes first mentioned in the 5th century. The Hungarians that settled in the Roman province of Pannonia between the 5th and 9th centuries were a medley of Turkish Onogurs and Ugric Magyars. The "H" that begins Hungary is a folk etymological association with the Huns. The medieval Latin term "*Hungarus*" first appears in the 8th century.

Relatively few Hungarian words have filtered into English. This is not surprising, as Hungarian is not a member of the Indo-European group of languages which represents the largest language family in the world.

Hungarian, along with Finnish, Estonian, and Lapp, represents the Finno-Ugric language family which is spoken by approximately 23 million people in the world. Around 3000 B.C., the Ugrians left their ancestral home in the Ural Mountains and migrated in a southerly direction to the Tobol and Irtis river basins, which are now situated in Siberia and Kazakhstan. Between the 5th and 9th centuries A.D. they were forced to migrate westward and they eventually reached the Danube where they settled in 896 A.D. In the more than a thousand years that have elapsed since that time, the Hungarians became completely Europeanized, with only their language serving to reveal their Asian lineage.

The Hungarian-Finnish link is apparent in some words. "Blood" is rendered as "*veri*" in Finnish and as "*vér*" in Hungarian; "hand" is "*kasi*" in Finnish and "*kéz*" in Hungarian; "honey" is "*mesi*" in Finnish and "*mez*" in Hungarian; and "to go" is rendered as "*menna*" in Finnish and as "*menni*" in Hungarian. Usually, however, the words in the two languages have drifted further apart. The word "three" in Finnish is "*kolme,*" and in Hungarian "*három*;" "eye" is "*silma*" in Finnish and "*szem*" in Hungarian, and "horn" is "*sarvi*" in Finnish and "*sarv*" in Hungarian.

There is one community in the world where Finns and Hungarians still live side by side. It is neither in Finland nor Hungary, but in Fairfield, Ohio (population 4,500), a Finnish-Hungarian settlement thrives, and two ancient peoples have the opportunity of reuniting the Finno-Ugric language family.

Many of the English words descended from Hungarian relate to Hungarian history and culture. The word "hussar" ("Hungarian cavalry member") comes from "*huszar,*" which originally referred to a freebooter; only later did it come to describe a horseman. The word probably comes from "*husz*" ("twenty") and "*ár*" ("price"), as these men were paid twenty units of currency for enlisting. "Csardas" is a Hungarian dance composed of a slow section followed by a faster one, and its name derives from the word "*csárda*" ("inn"). "Tzigane" comes from the Magyar "*cigány*" and refers to a Gypsy. A "shako" is a tall cylindrical military hat; the word comes from "*csákó,*" which is a shortened version of "*csákó suveg*" ("peaked cap"). "Soutache" is a corruption of the Hungarian "*szuszak*" ("a pendant curl of hair"). In English, it refers to a narrow flat ornamental braid of wool, silk, or the like, usually sewn upon fabrics in fanciful designs.

Hungarian towns have given their names to several words in our language. The Hungaran town of Vizsla has bequeathed us the dog known as the "vizsla," a golden-brown pointer with large ears. We also have Tokay wine, a rich sweet wine of an aromatic flavour, made near Tokay in Hungary. The term "Tokay wine" is also applied to a Californian wine made in imitation of this, and similarly to an Australian vine, grape, and white wine.

Not too many readers will be familiar with Dobos Torte, a rich cake made of alternate layers of sponge and chocolate or mocha cream, with a crisp caramel topping, named after 19th-century Hungarian pastry chef József Dobos. But eveyone knows the Hungarian pair of "goulash" and "paprika." "Goulash" comes from "*gulyás(hús)*" with "*gulyás*" meaning "herdsman" and "*hús*" meaning "meat." "Paprika" was absorbed into Hungarian from Serbo-Croatian, in which "*pàpar*" refers to "pepper."

[Italian]

Next to Latin, French, and the Scandinavian languages, the language from which English has absorbed the greatest number of words is Italian. Many words of Italian origin are easy to spot because they end with the vowels "a," "i," or "o." In this category we have "belladonna," "broccoli," "casino," "confetti," "embargo," fiasco," "macaroni," (the anglicized version of "*maccheroni*"), "pizza," "rotunda," "torso," "vendetta," and "volcano." The field of music abounds with words of Italian origin. Examples include "aria," "baritone," "cantata," "concerto," "falsetto," "opera," "piano," "sonata," "soprano," "stanza," "trombone," and "violin" (from "*violino*").

But not all English words of Italian descent are as transparent in displaying their pedigree. The word "ballot," for example, is derived from the Italian "*ballotta*" ("little ball"). In days of yore, people voted by dropping little balls into a receptacle. The first *OED* citation, from 1561, states, "Boxes into whiche if he wyll, he may let fall his ballot, that no man can perceiue hym." Since a white ball often meant a "yes" vote and a black ball designated a "no" vote, the term "blackball" has come to refer to undesirability.

"Bankrupt" is another word of Italian lineage. It comes from the Italian "*bancarotta*," which means "bank broken" or "bench broken." In the 16th century the word "bankrupt" was often rendered as "banke rota." The first *OED* citation, from *State Papers, Henry VIII* in 1539, says: "With danger to make with banke rota." In medieval times, and possibly even thousands of years earlier, moneylenders would transact their business on a small bench. According to Samuel Johnson, "It is said that when an Italian money-changer became insolvent his 'bench was broke.'" Another "bank" word of Italian lineage is the word "mountebank," usually replaced nowadays by the inelegant-sounding "quack." "Mountebank" comes from the Italian word "*montambanco,*" which is itself a contraction of "*monta in banco*" ("mount on bench"). Quacks historically often sold their wares at fairs by mounting a bench to deliver their spiel.

The *OED* states that a "gambit" is "a method of opening the game, in which with the sacrifice of a pawn or piece the player seeks to obtain some advantage over his opponent," and says that the word comers from the Italian "*gambetto*" ("tripping up the heels" in wrestling). "*Gambetto*" itself derives from "*gamba*" ("leg"), and it was borrowed into Spanish as "*gambito,*" where the notion of an "underhanded procedure" was first applied to a chess manoeuvre in 1561.

In the last four centuries the vocabularies of music, and to a lesser extent art, have been the greatest beneficiaries of words of Italian origin. Surprisingly, however, the field to which English owes the greatest portion of its early Italian loans is the military.

One of the earliest loan-words from Italian is "alarm," which came into English in 1393. If we are alarmed, we should spring to arms because that is what the Italian "*all' arme*" meant. Later the Italians rendered it as "*allarme*" and over time the sense of the word shifted from a military command to the sense of panic one experienced on hearing this clarion call. Nowadays, we often think of "alarm" in the context of an alarm clock. This sense even pervaded the 17th century; in 1665, diarist Samuel Pepys wrote, "And so to bed, to be up betimes by the helpe of a larum watch."

The bulk of the Italian military words surfaced in our language in the 16th century. The earliest sense of the word "squadron" is "a body of soldiers drawn up or arranged in a square formation." The word comes from the Italian "*squadrone,*" which comes from the word "*squadra*" ("square"). "Colonel" comes from the Italian "*colonello,*" which is related to the word "*colonna*" ("column"). This is because the colonel would lead the column at the head of a regiment.

"Rocket" derives from the Italian "*rocchetta,*" which itself comes from the Italan "*rocca*" ("rock"). "Pistol" comes from the word "*pistolet,*" which originally referred to a 15th-century dagger made in Pistoia, Tuscany. Later, small guns were made in Pistoia and the town is still noted for metalwork and gun-making. The *OED* shows an obsolete sense of "musket" as the "male of the sparrowhawk." Musket comes to us by way of the French *mousquet* which came from the Italian "*moschetto*," "sparrowhawk." This follows the practice of naming types of firearms after a bird of prey.

A military word of Italian lineage that reaches our language later than one would think is the word "attack." It comes from the Italian "*attaccare*" and its first *OED* citations are as a verb from 1600 and as a noun from 1667. The *OED* notes that "attack" is absent from the works of Shakespeare and appears only once in the works of Milton in 1667. The word "attack" unites the disparate fields of the military and music; one of the senses of "attack" noted in the *OED*, is "the action of beginning a piece, passage, or phrase, in respect of precision and clarity." So much for a quiet night at the symphony. Ciao.

[Portuguese]

Some languages get short etymological shrift. Like the Celtic languages, the Portuguese contribution to English is sometimes underestimated. Typical is the following passage in *The Origins and Development of the English Language* by American linguist Thomas Pyles: "No words came into English direct from Portuguese until the modern period: those which have been adopted include albino, flamingo, madeira (from the place), molasses, pagoda, palaver and pickaninny (pequenino, 'very small')."

However, Pyles has omitted several words of clear Portuguese lineage. "Coconut" derives from the Portuguese and Spanish "*coco,*" which in turn comes from the Latin. The plural form "*coquos*" is quoted first from the *Roteiro de Vasco da Gama* of 1498. The word "coco" in Portuguese and Spanish means "grinning face." The fruit is called "coconut" because when Portuguese explorers first saw this fruit in the Indian Ocean islands they fancied that the little indentations at the base of the nut resembled eyes. The first *OED* citation is from 1555. It states, "This frute was cauled Cocus for this cause, that, when it is taken from the place where it cleaueth ... there are seene two holes."

The *OED* shows a multilinguistic etymology for the word "buffalo": "Italian *buffalo* or Portuguese *búfalo* from the vulgar Latin *bufalus*." It explains that the Latin term most likely descended from a similar-sounding Greek word. It adds, however that "the early quotations suggest that the word originally came into English from Portuguese." The first citation, from 1588, is a translation of J. Gonzalez de Mendoza's *Historie of the Great and Mightie Kingdome of China*: "They doo plough and till their ground with kine, Bufalos, and bulles." Another animal term emanating from Portuguese is "dodo." The first citation of "dodo" is from 1628: "A strange fowle, which I had at the Iland mauritius, called ... a DoDo." This extinct cerebrally and evolutionary challenged bird received its name from the Portuguese "*doudo*" ("simpleton, fool"). Another word from Portuguese is "marmalade" from "*marmelada*." It was, however, absorbed into English via the French "*marmelade*."

In many cases it is difficult to determine whether a word came into English from Portuguese or Spanish. The word "apricot" was adopted either from the Portuguese "*albricoque*" or the Spanish "*albaricoque*." As noted above it ultimately derives from the Arabic "*al-burqkq*." The first English citation, dated 1551, states that "abrecockes ... are less than the other peches." But by the 18th century it changed from "apricock" to "apricot." Similarly, the word "masquerade" comes from either the Portuguese "*mascarar*" or the Catalan "*mascarar*," and ultimately from the Arabic "*maskhara*" ("laughing-stock, buffoon").

Actually, Pyles' short list of "direct" Portuguese words isn't necessarily so direct. "Albino" is also a word in Spanish. The *OED* relates that the term was applied by the Portuguese "to white Negroes on the coast of Africa." The *OED* defines a "pickaninny" as "a little one, a child" and adds that the word "which often gives offence when used by people of European extraction refers in the West Indies and America to children of Black African ethnic origin." "Pickaninny" derives from the word "*pequeño*," which exists in both Portuguese and Spanish. The claim can be made that "flamenco" came direct from the Spanish "*flamenco*" rather than the Portuguese "*flamengo*." And can it be stated definitively that the word "molasses" really drives from the Portuguese "*melaço*" when there exists the Italian "*melazzo*," and before that the Latin "*mellceum*" ("of the nature of honey")?

The *OED* defines "palaver" as "a talk, parley, conference, discussion: chiefly applied to conferences, with much talk, between African or other tribespeople, and traders or travellers." It relates that the word "*palavra*" appears to have been used by Portuguese traders on the coast of Africa for a talk or colloquy with the natives where it was picked up by English sailors and passed from nautical slang into colloquial use. Its first *OED* citation is taken from John Atkins' 1735 *Voyage to Guinea*: "He found it as the fetish man had said, and a Palaaver being called, Peter recovered two ounces of gold damage." "Pagoda" derives from the Portuguese "*pagoda*" but may be a corruption of a name found by the Portuguese in India. Some etymologists believe that "pagoda" ultimately derives from the Persian "*but-kadah*" ("idol-temple").

It is often impossible to trace the exact etymology of English words and we see this pattern in some words of Portuguese lineage. The fish "grouper" in Portuguese is "*garupa*," but this might come out of an indigenous language in South America. A "yam" may derive from the Portuguese "*inhame*" or the Spanish "*igname*," but the *OED* says "ultimate origin unknown."

In the modern era we have derived many dance names from Portuguese. The *OED* relates that "samba" is "Portuguese of African origin." Strangely, its first citation is from W. Moberly's 1885 *The Rocks and Rivers of British Columbia*: "It was here I first saw the graceful South American dance—the zemba queca." The year 1962 saw the addition of the dance "bossa nova" to our vocabulary. "*Bossa*" in Portuguese means "tendency" and "*nova*" means "new." Making its *OED* debut in 1997 was the "lambada," which in Portuguese literally means "beating, lashing," deriving from the verb "*lambar*" ("to beat, whip"). The first citation is from the *Financial Times* of 1988: "São Paulo's current cultural explosion is the lambada, a lithe, lascivious Caribbean dance that first arrived in the 1930s and was banned by the then-government as obscene."

[Russian]

On November 9, 1989, the border separating Western and Eastern Germany was opened, but cracks in the wall of Communism were appearing by the mid-'80s. Just as Communism was set to implode, the English language was invaded by a pair of Russian words. It all started in 1979 at the 26th Communist Party Congress, where it was proposed to reform the Soviet economic and political systems. The word used to describe this process was "*perestroika*," which literally means "restructuring" in Russian. By 1986, "perestroika" is recorded in the *OED*. Also making its *OED* debut in 1986 was "glasnost," which referred to a declared Soviet policy for greater openness in public statements, including the publication of news reflecting adversely on the government and the political system. As a result of this policy, greater freedom of speech became tolerated. The word "*glasnost*" in Russian literally means "the fact of being public" and is first recorded in the Russian vocabulary in the 18th century, but with the more general sense of "publicity."

"Perestroika" and "glasnost" are typical of Russian words that have trickled into English but have never become fully integrated. Usually, when English adopts words from other languages, these words become firmly embedded in our language and lose their foreign flavour. Most Russian words that have seeped into English have not become totally naturalized into our language and remain cocooned in a Russian cosmos. Observe "soviet," "commissar," "troika," "apparatchik," "gulag," "samovar," "steppe," "babushka," "Bolshevik," "dacha," "samizdat," and "pogrom." The last two words bear some explanation. "Samizdat" is actually an abbreviation of "*samoizdatel stvo*" ("self-publishing house") and came into English in the 1960s to refer to the clandestine or illegal copying of literature. "Pogrom" means "devastation" in Russian and the *OED* defines it as "an organized massacre in Russia for the destruction or annihilation of any body or class: originally and especially applied to those directed against the Jews."

Some words of Russian origin that have been digested by the English language have found a passageway through foods associated with Jews. *The Jewish Encyclopedia* published in 1903 states that "the kasha and blintzes of the Russian Jews are dishes adopted by the Jews from their Gentile neighbors." "Blintze" is an adaptation of the Russian "*blinets*," which is a diminutive of the word "*blin*" ("pancakes"). In Jewish cookery, a latke is a pancake, usually made with grated potato. Its name derives from the Russian "*látka*" ("pastry"). In Jewish North American cuisine, a "knish" is a piece of baked or fried dough filled with meat, cheese, or potato. The word derives from the Russian "*knysh*" (a kind of cake). However, the Russian influence on Yiddish transcends words for food. Observe "*nudnik*," a Yiddish word meaning "pesterer." It blends the Russian "*núdnyi*" ("tedious, boring") with the suffix "-*nik*," which has also bequeathed us "sputnik" from the Russian "*sputnik*" ("travelling companion"), "refusenik" from the Russian "*otkáznik*," and "beatnik." The Yiddish word "*tsatske*" (sometimes rendered as "*tchotchke*" or "*chachka*") is used in English to refer to an inexpensive trinket, and sometimes to a pretty girl, and derives from either the Russian "*tsatska*" or the Polish "*czaczko*."

Certain words connected with northern climes also have a Russian connection. For example, the word "parka" refers to a long jacket with a hood attached, designed for Arctic conditions and traditionally worn by the Inuit and Aleut peoples. This word comes from the Russian word for "skin jacket." "Tundra" refers to topographically flat regions that contain Arctic climate and vegetation with the word coming via Russian from the Lappish "*tundar*."

Of course, some English words of Russian lineage have totally transcended their boundaries. While it is debatable whether "vodka," from the Russian "*vódka*" (pronounced "*votka*") is fully acclimatized into our language, no debate is possible with some other words of Russian descent. The main sense of the word "mammoth" is "enormous," but the word was first applied to the large hairy elephant of the genus "*Mammuthus.*" Skeletons of this extinct animal were found in Siberia in 1706. The word derives from the Russian "*mammot,*" which may derive from a Siberian language in which the word meant "earth" or "soil." The *OED* relates that while "sable" comes from the Old French "*sable*" or "*saible,*" this word was probably adopted from the Russian "*sobol.*" The fish "beluga" is also of Russian lineage; "*belo*" (as in "Belorussia") means "white." While "tsar" or "czar" was adopted into English from Russian, the word can be traced back further. It came into Russian from the old Slavic word "*cesare*" which itself is derived from "Caesar." Etymologically, the word "*tsar*" is also connected to the word "*kaiser.*"

Russian has been cited as a possible source of English words that carry unpleasant connotations. For example, the *OED* relates that the term "disinformation," the dissemination of deliberately false information, may derive from the Russian "*dezinformatsiya.*"

[Spanish]

By the middle of the 19th century, large swaths of Mexico had become part of the United States. Small wonder then that the English language absorbed a large number of Spanish words by 1850. There is a frontier atmosphere to the words that are absorbed in this period: "bonanza," "bronco," "buckaroo," "canyon," "gaucho," "gringo," "lariat," "ranch," "rodeo," "stampede," "vamoose," and "vigilante," among others.

In the 20th century, many of the words that English has borrowed from Spanish have served to spice up our lives, sometimes literally. In

1949, when I was less than one year old and unable to enjoy solid foods, the trio of "taco," "nacho," and "jalapeño" began to liven up the pages of the *OED*. The journal *American Speech* reported that "the touristas almost always eat in a Mexican restaurant and bravely attempt to order their meals in Spanish. Such meals are *tækoz,* a mispronunciation of the Spanish word *tacos.*" The OED relates that "nacho" probably derives from the abbreviation of the name of Mexican chef, Ignacio Anaya, who is often credited with creating the first "nacho." A publication of the *Church of the Redeemer* in Eagle Pass, Texas, reported in 1970 that "this simple yet delicious snack originated some years ago in the Old Victory Club in Piedras Negras, Mexico, when a group of Eagle Pass women asked the chef, Nacho, to make something for them to eat with their cocktails." The word "jalapeño" derives from the town of Jalapa, Mexico, whence this hot, green chilli pepper comes. The 1940s also brought us "tostada," a deep-fried cornmeal pancake topped with a seasoned mixture of beans, mincemeat, and vegetables. The word derives from the past participle of the verb "*tostar*" ("to toast"). The 1940s also brought into English the "quesadilla," a variety of turnover, usually with a cheese filling.

Making its debut in the 1930s is "burrito," which is a diminutive of the word "*burro*" ("ass"). The 1920s brought us "guacamole," but the etymology for this word belongs to another language. It comes from the Nahuatl word "*ahuacamolli,*" which blends "*ahuacatl*" ("avocado") with "*molli*" ("sauce").

All the above can be washed down with "sangria," a drink of red wine, fruit juice, carbonated water, sugar, and brandy or another liquor, usually served in a jug with pieces of fruit. Ultimately this word derives from the Latin "*sanguis*" ("blood") from which English derives the word "sanguine."

Recently the *OED* updated its listings of Mexican foods. "Fajita" was added in 2002. A fajita consists of beef or chicken that has been marinated, grilled, cut into strips, and served in a small tortilla. It derives from Mexican Spanish, where it means "little strip" or "belt." Still not represented in the *OED*, however, is "chimichanga." This is a fried burrito containing a spicy meat filling. In Mexican Spanish this word means "trinket."

The 20th century also saw an explosion of Spanish dances into our language. "Flamenco" and "tango" made their *OED* debut at the turn of the 20th century. The *OED* entry for "tango," which the dictionary defines as "a Spanish flamenco dance," cites its initial appearance in H.C. Chatfield-

Taylor's *Land of of the Castanet* (1896): "The girls ... dance again, not the vulgar flamenco or tango, but the charming dance of the province." The first citation of "rumba" is from J. Hergesheimer's *Bright Shawl* in 1922: "Her life was incredibly, wildly, debauched. Among other things, she danced, as the mulata, the rumba, an indescribable affair." The year 1935 brought us "conga" (pertaining to the Congo), and the following year "merengue" appeared in our lexicon. In 1948, "mambo" appears. The *OED* states that it comes from American Spanish, probably from Haitian Creole. Also coming from American Spanish is "cha-cha." The first citation in the *OED* is from the British musical newsweekly *Melody Maker* in 1954: "What Touzet means by 'cha-cha', as far as I can make out, is simply a mambo with a pronounced güiro rhythm." Surprisingly, "*macareña*" has not yet been included in the *OED*.

Assorted Spanish words and expressions have also served to enliven our language. The first use in English of the term "olé" occurs in the aforementioned 1922 *Bright Shawl*. "Hasta la vista" is first recorded in English in 1935. Not surprisingly, the first citation of the word "cojones" ("testicles," "guts") is from a work by Ernest Hemingway. In his 1932 novel *Death in the Afternoon* he writes, "It takes more cojones to be a sportsman where death is a closer party to the game."

One of the most intoxicating Spanish imports into our language is "marijuana," first recorded (with a variant spelling) in *Scribner's Magazine* in 1894: "Toloachi and mariguan ... are used by discarded women for the purpose of wreaking a terrible revenge upon recreant lovers." "Mescaline," ultimately from the Spanish "*mezcal*," joined our vocabulary in 1896.

[Turkish]

The star attraction of Thanksgiving dinner received its name in an unwarranted manner. "Turkey" figures into the name because the fowl had originally been imported into Europe from territory that the Europeans thought was Turkish. The *OED* cites its use in a text from 1655: "They were first brought from Numidia into Turky, and thence to Europe, whereupon they were called Turkies."

There are other delights of Turkish lineage for us to savour. Many of them came into English between the beginning and middle of the 17th century.

The *OED* records "caviar" as first appearing in English in 1591; it apparently comes from the Turkish "*khavyar*," though the *OED* points out "It has no root in Turkish, and has not the look of a Turkish word." "Sherbet" joins our lexicon in 1603 and comes from a Turkish and Persian word of the same spelling which comes from the Arabic "*shariba*," "to drink." The first *OED* definition of sherbet is "a cooling drink of the East, made of fruit juice and water, sweetened, often cooled with snow." This is borne out in its first citation from the 1603 *History Turkes*: "The guests dranke water prepared with sugar, which kind of drink they call Zerbet." The word "pilaf" is recorded by the *OED* as dating from 1612 in English. A citation from *Travels of Four Englishmen* states, "The most common dish [amongst the Turks] is Pilaw ... made of Rice and small morsels of Mutton boiled therein." "Yogurt" joins our vocabulary in 1625, coming from the same word in Turkish. The *OED* offers a citation from 1625: "Neither doe they [the Turks] eate much Milke, except it bee made sower, which they call Yoghurd." The dessert dish "baklava," made from thin pieces of flaky pastry, honey, and nuts, was absorbed from Turkish in 1653.

"Coffee" also was absorbed from Turkish where it was pronounced "*kahveh*." In Arabic, it is rendered as "*qahwah*," and some Arab lexicographers claim that it originally meant "wine" and is a derivative of the verb "*qahiya*" ("to have no appetite"). There are several colourful legends about the origin of coffee. One of these claims that around 850 A.D., a goatherd named Kaldi became puzzled as to the frenetic behaviour of his flock after they had eaten certain berries. Not one to act sheepishly, Kaldi tried these berries himself and felt a sense of exhilaration afterwards. He then rushed off to tell his fellow goatherds about the bush with the buzz. The Arabs soon learned to dry and boil the berries, and called the concoction "*qahwe*" or "*qahwah*." Some lexicographers believe that the ultimate etymology is African and that the word comes from the district of Kaffa in the south Abyssinian highlands, where the plant appears to be native. In any case, the European languages generally appear to have got the name from Turkish "*kahveh*," around 1600. The *OED* cites an appearance in English in 1598 in *Linschoten's Travels*, which features a peculiar rendition of the word "coffee": "The Turkes holde almost the same manner of drinking of their Chaoua, which they make of a certaine fruit ... by the Egyptians called Bon or Ban."

Since the 17th century there has been a marked decline in the food words that English has absorbed from Turkish. One word that was absorbed in the last century, however, was "shish kebab," which we adopted in 1914 from the Turkish "*siskebap*," which combines the elements "*sis*" ("skewer") with "*kebap*" ("roast meat"). The *OED* also says that the name of the Greek dish tzatziki, consisting of yogurt with chopped cucumber and garlic, comes from Turkish.

English has absorbed other words from Turkish, often with the sense of the word shifting over time. Most dictionaries define a "divan" as a type of backless sofa, but its original sense from Turkish was rather different. The *OED* relates that in the late 16th century it referred to "an Oriental council of state; specifically in Turkey, the privy council ... presided over by the Sultan, or in his absence by the grand vizier."

Unlike a turkey, the name of the jackal is of true Turkish lineage, as the word is a corruption of the Turkish "*chakl.*" This doesn't mean, however, that I recommend replacing Turkey Day with the Day of the Jackal.

7

The Asian and African Connection

[Chinese]

I asked this question recently to ten people: "Can you name an English word that comes from Chinese?" Not surprisingly, the responses sounded like a Chinese restaurant take-out order: four chow meins, three chop sueys, two won tons and one dim sum. The first word in this grouping to make it into the *OED* was "chop suey," an adaptation of the Cantonese "*shap sui*" ("mixed bits") which is first recorded in English in 1888. Actually, the "chop" in chopsticks also has a Chinese origin, but here the meaning is "quick." "Chopsticks" is a corruption of "*k'wâi-tsze*," "the quick and nimble ones." "Chow mein" is first recorded in 1903, and "won ton" and "dim sum" in 1948.

Chinese has been nourishing us with food words for centuries. "Tofu" joined our lexicon in 1880. The word is rendered in Chinese as "*dòufu*"; "*dòu*" means "beans" and "*fu*" means "rotten." Tofu is made from a soybean extract and the word "soy" (or "soya") is a 17th-century Chinese extract. It comes from the word "*shi-yu;*" "*shi*" in Chinese means "salted beans" and "*yu*" means "oil." Joining our language around the same time is the fruit "kumquat," which in Chinese is rendered as "*kin kü*" ("gold orange").

The word "ketchup" starts to flavour our language early in the 18th century and is generally seen as deriving from the Malay "*kechap.*" But this word itself comes from the word "*kêtsiap*" in the Chinese Amoy dialect, where it refers to "pickled fish-brine" or "sauce." The original condiment that Dutch traders imported from Asia appears to have been a fish sauce or a sauce made from special mushrooms salted for preservation. A citation from 1711 in the *OED* states, "Soy comes in tubbs from Japan and the best ketchup from Tonquin, yet goods of both sorts are made and sold very cheap in China." The English added a "t" to the Malay word, changed the "a" to a "u" and started making ketchup themselves, using ingredients like mushrooms, walnuts, cucumbers, and oysters. It wasn't until American seamen added tomatoes from Mexico or the Spanish West Indies that the quintessential tomato ketchup was born.

Whereas Arabic brought us intoxicating beverages such as alcohol and coffee, Chinese can take credit for an inebriating libation—tea. British slang for a cup of tea is "cuppa char," "char" being a corruption of *"cha"* ("tea"), which derives from the Mandarin *"ch'a"* for the same. This is reflected in the *OED* source example, a 1598 mention with the spelling "chaa;" its first mention in Europe is as "cha" in Portugal in 1559. Under the name *"te"* or *"thee,"* it was imported by the Dutch from Java, where it had been brought by Chinese merchants from the province of Amoy. Tea was introduced in France in 1635, Russia in 1638, and England around 1655. Tea was first sold publicly in England at Garway's Coffee House in London; in 1660, Samuel Pepys recorded in his diary, "I did send for a cup of tee (a China drink) of which I never had drank before."

Over the next two centuries, Chinese bequeathed to English a variety of tea words. "Pekoe" is described by the *OED* as "a superior kind of black tea so-called from the leaves being picked young with the down still on them." It came into our language in 1712 from the Chinese *"peh-ho," "peh"* meaning "white" and *"ho"* referring to "down." The black tea "souchong" made its English debut in 1760, deriving from the word *"siao-chung"* ("small sort"). "Oolong" is a mid-19th-century addition that derives from *"wu-lung," "wu"* referring to "black" and *"lung"* meaning "dragon."

Chinese contributions to English transcend our palates. The rhyming words "tycoon" and "typhoon," for example, are both of Chinese vintage. "Tycoon" ultimately comes from the Chinese words *"ta"* ("great") and *"kiun"* ("prince"). It was adopted in Japanese as *"taikun"* ("great lord") and was the title by which the shogun would be described to foreigners. "Typhoon" comes from the words *"ta"* ("big") and *"feng"* ("wind").

The word "kowtow" in English bears a taint of obsequiousness, but its origin in Chinese doesn't connote an act of servility. It comes from the words *"k'o"* ("knock") and *"t'ou"* ("the head") and derives from the Chinese custom of touching the ground with the forehead as an expression of extreme respect. The word "gung-ho" comes from the words *"kung"* ("work") and *"ho"* ("together"). It was adopted in World War II by U.S. Marines under the command of General Evans Carlson. The November 8, 1942 *New York Times* reported that "borrowing an idea from China, Carlson frequently has what he calls kung-hou meetings. ... [P]roblems are threshed out and orders explained." Probably owing to the practice of some Marines in showing the same enthusiasm in picayune matters such as white glove inspections, the term "gung-ho" acquired a connotation of "overzealousness."

Chinese place names commemorated in English words tend to have a strong culinary bent. Observe "Szechuan," "Cantonese," and "Peking Duck."

The verb "to shanghai" is defined as "to drug or otherwise render insensible, and ship on board a vessel wanting hands." This is fairly harsh treatment on a slow boat to or from China, but given my druthers, I'd rather be shanghaied than "bobbitized."

[Indian Languages]

In 1783, during the early days of the Raj, Sir William Jones was appointed Chief Justice in India. Jones took it upon himself to learn Sanskrit in order to fully understand Hindu and Muslim laws. Four years later, he observed that the Sanskrit language, whatever be its antiquity, is of a wonderful structure; more perfect than the Greek, more copious than the Latin and more exquisitely refined than either, yet bearing to both of them a stronger affinity, both in the roots of verbs, and in the forms of grammar, than could possibly have been produced by accident; so strong indeed, that no philosopher could examine them all without believing them to have sprung from some common source which perhaps no longer exists.

Jones' linguistic analysis also highlighted the similarity between Sanskrit and the Germanic and Celtic language groups.

For almost two millennia, Sanskrit, which means "well-formed, perfected," has been maintained as the literary language of the priestly and learned castes in India and it maintains this position in the 21st century.

The western world's Sanskrit legacy is apparent in many kinship words. The Sanskrit word for "father" is "*pitr*," similar to the Greek and Latin "*pater*;" "mother" in Sanskrit is "*matr*," almost identical to Latin "*mater*." Sanskrit "*bhratr*" became Old English "*bodor*," German, Swedish, and Danish "*broder*," and modern English "brother." "*Svasa*" in Sanskrit bequeathed us the Old English "*sweoster*," the German "*schwester*" and the modern English "sister." "Son" in Sanskrit is "*sunu*"; "daughter" is "*duhitar*."

Sanskrit has also bequeathed us some words for numbers. The number "two" in Sanskrit was rendered as "*dwau*," which became the Old English "*twá*" and the Dutch "*twee*"; "three" in Sanskrit is "*trayas*," and in Norwegian, Swedish, and Danish "*tre*" and the Dutch "*drie*." The number "four" in Sanskrit is "*catvar*," quite similar to the Latin "*quattuor*" and the Old Irish "*cethir*."

It is not surprising that Sanskrit has bequeathed religious words to many languages, including English. "Nirvana" refers to a state of spiritual enlightenment that involves the freeing of the self; it derives from the Sanskrit "*nirva*" ("blowing out, extinction, disappearance"). A "mantra" is a holy word or phrase that is repeated in meditation; in Sanskrit it means "instrument of thought" and comes from the verb "*man*" ("to think"). "Yoga" in Sanskrit means "union" and, etymologically, it is connected with the word "yoke," which refers to a not particularly spiritual union, the coupling of oxen. Gandhi's title "Mahatma" comes from the Sanskrit "*mahtman*" ("great-souled"). The word "avatar" is often used to refer to the embodiment of something, but originally it referred to the incarnation of a Hindu God. It comes from the Sanskrit "*avatara*" ("descent") and it blends the Sanskrit words "*ava*" ("down") and "*tra*" ("to pass over"). "Karma" in Sanskrit designates "action" or "fate."

Sanskrit's legacy to English transcends religion and has also literally sweetened our language. The troops of Alexander the Great enjoyed a Persian delicacy which was composed of a sweet reed garnished with honey, spices, and colouring. This Persian treat was called "*kand*" and this word derived from the old Arabic word for "sugar," "*quand*." Ultimately, candy comes from the Sanskrit "*khanda*," "piece of something," or "sugar in crystalline pieces."

Sanskrit has also given us the word "anil," the West Indian shrub with small reddish yellow flowers that is the source of the indigo dye. It is, however, the blue colour that figures in the etymology, as "*nila*" in Sanskrit means "dark blue." This passed into Persian as "*nil*," from which "*nilak*" was derived. This, in turn, passed into Arabic as "*lilak*," whence we derived "lilac."

Probably the most notorious word we have absorbed from Sanskrit is "swastika," which ironically is a marriage of "*sú*" ("good") and "*asti*" ("being"). This is a word for an ancient good-luck symbol, deriving from the Sanskrit "*svasti*" ("well-being, fortune, luck"). The first definition for "swastika" in the *OED* is "a primitive symbol or ornament of the form of a cross with equal arms with a limb of the same length projecting at right angles from the end of each arm, all in the same direction and (usually) clockwise." The symbol was adopted by the Nazi Party and in German was referred to as the "*Hakenkreuz*." A 1932 citation states that "Thousands flocked to his standard—the 'Hakenkreuz' (swastika)—the ancient anti-semitic cross in a colour scheme of red-white-black in memory of the colors of the old army." It is the karma of Sanskrit to have provided us both the sweetness of "candy" and the bitterness of "swastika."

As India may have as many as ninety million people who are reasonably fluent in English, it should be of no surprise that many of the new words that are flooding into English come from India. Some new entries include: "mahar" (member of a caste of western India, whose duties include village watchman and public messenger) and "mahajan" ("moneylender").

One doesn't have to limit oneself to obscure words when it comes to words of South Asian origin that have joined our lexicon. India is home to twenty-four languages, each spoken by at least one million people. The adoption by English of many words from these languages serves as a case study on how meanings become generalized upon their immigration into our language.

The *OED* advises that

> the pundit of the Supreme Court (in India) was a Hindu officer, whose duty it was to advise the English judges when needful on questions of Hindu law. … In Anglo-Indian use, pundit was applied also to a native Indian trained in the use of instruments and employed to survey regions beyond the British frontier and inaccessible to Europeans.

Currently, the word is usually applied to someone who acts as a critic or authority on a particular subject, especially in the media.

The description of "thug" in the *OED* makes it sound like a ghoulish tax-deductible organization: "Association of professional robbers and murderers in India who strangled their victims." The actual name of this fraternal order was "P'hanisigars" ("noose operators") and the British euphemistically bequeathed them the name "Thugs," from the Sanskrit word "*sthaga*," meaning "cheater," which dates at least to the 13th century. The Thugs were said to be honouring the Hindu goddess of destruction, Kali, through their mayhem. The British liquidated the Thugs in the 1830s, when they hanged over five hundred of them and sentenced close to three thousand to life imprisonment. The word "thug" lives on with the sense of one inclined or hired to treat another roughly or brutally.

"Pariah" is another word whose meaning became generalized over time. The *OED* states that a pariah was a "member of a very extensive low caste (the Paraiyars) in Southern India, especially numerous in Madras, where its members supplied most of the domestics in European service." The name derives from the Tamil "*parai*" ("large drum") because the duty of the Paraiyars was to beat the drum at certain religious festivals. The British, incorrectly believing that the Paraiyars represented the lowest caste, adopted the word "pariah" to refer to any social outcast.

The term "guru" has similarly gone from having a specific to a more general meaning. It entered our language in 1613 to refer to a Hindu spiritual teacher, but in the 20th century it acquired the generalized sense of "mentor." This is reflected in two *OED* citations: in 1949 we have Arthur Koestler stating, "My self-confidence as a Guru had gone," and in 1967, there was a comment in the magazine *New Scientist* that "Marshall McLuhan is one of those gurus whom the United States hungers for more than other nations."

The word "juggernaut" is now employed metaphorically to refer to a "crushing force," but originally the "crush" was literal. In Hinduism, "*Jagganath*" is a title of the god Krishna. The *OED* states that "the idol of this deity at Puri [in India] [is] annually dragged in procession on an enormous car, under the wheels of which many devotees are said to have formerly thrown themselves to be crushed."

We see similar changes in the meanings of names for objects. In India, a "*bangl*" is a one-story thatched or tiled house surrounded by a veranda. Its name literally means "of Bengal," where such houses are common. The British in India borrowed the word, which eventually became "bungalow," and this word has come to describe any one-storied house. "Veranda" itself seems to have been introduced from India, as it is present in several languages in India, such as the Hindi "*varand*" and Bengali "*brand.*"

"Jungle" was originally rendered in Hindi and Marathia as "*jangal*" and meant "desert" or "waste." The same metamorphosis in meaning has occurred with the word "forest," which also referred to an unenclosed tract or waste before taking on the sense of "area covered with wood."

If you massage your scalp when you give yourself a "shampoo," you are performing the proper etymological activity. "Shampoo" comes from the Hindi word "*ampo*", the imperative of "*cmpn*" ("to press"). The first sense recorded in the *OED* is "to subject (a person, his limbs) to massage."

The first citation, dating from 1762, reflects an activity less sedentary than what we associate with hair salons: "Had I not seen several China merchants shampooed before me, I should have been apprehensive of danger." The ordinary sense of "shampoo" as "the washing of hair" emerges in the mid-19th century.

Of course, not every word we've adopted from South Asia has altered its meaning. "Pajamas" is Persian and Urdu for "leg-garment," from "*pë*" ("leg") and "*jmah*" ("clothing"). The *OED* describes pajamas as "loose ... trousers ... tied round the waist, worn by both sexes in Turkey, Iran and India."

[Japanese]

A website I visited advises tourists to Japan on how to communicate in Japanese concerning accommodation. "*Shinguru ruumu o hitori de ippaku onegai shimasu*" means "I would like a single room for one person for one night" and "*Kono hoteru ni wa puuru ga animasu ka?*" inquires, "Does this hotel have a swimming pool?" Notice how the Japanese have adopted English words into Japanese: "*shinguru ruumu*" is an approximation of "single room" and "*hoteru*" and "*puuru*" are adaptations of "hotel" and "swimming pool," respectively. Japanese has taken in many English words in this fashion: "*terebi*" means "television"; "*masukomi*," "mass communications"; "*erekutoronikusu*" means "electronics," and "*purutoniumu*," "plutonium." Baseball ("*beisobohru*") is a fertile ground for English terms. "*Goro*" is a ground ball; "*droppu*," a sinker; "*getto-tsui*" refers to a double play ("get two"); and "*taimuri hitto*" is a clutch hit ("timely hit").

But just as we have imported many goods from Japan, similarly we have absorbed many Japanese words into our vernacular. The arts are represented by "haiku," a form of Japanese verse developed in the mid-16th century; a haiku consists of seventeen syllables and is usually of jesting character. From Japan we also have "origami," which blends the words "*ori*" ("fold") and "*kami*" ("paper"), as origami is the Japanese art of folding paper into intricate designs.

Probably no field is as dominated by Japanese loan-words as the martial arts. "Karate" blends the "*kara*" ("empty") and "*te*" ("hand"); "judo" is a combination of "*ju*" ("gentleness") and "*do*" ("way"); "ninja" combines "*nin*" ("stealth") and "*ja*" ("person"). Also in this domain we have "jujitsu," "aikido," "kendo," and "sumo."

Some Japanese words were popularized in English during the Second World War. The *OED* relates that a "kamikaze" was "one of the airmen who … made deliberate suicide crashes into enemy targets." The word literally means "wind of the gods." In Japanese lore, it refers to the supposed divine wind that blew on an August night in 1281, destroying the navy of the invading Mongols. The word "honcho" was imported from Japan by fliers stationed there during the occupation and during the Korean War. Originally, the word referred to a leader of a small group or squad and over time became generalized to refer to someone in charge of a situation.

Sometimes the Japanese words we've absorbed offer us a brief history of Japan. The *OED* defines "shogun" as "the hereditary commander-in-chief of the Japanese army until 1867 and the virtual ruler of Japan. By successive usurpations of power, the Shogun had become the real ruler of Japan, though nominally the subject of the Mikado, and acting in his name." "Shogun" is a shortened form of "*sei-i-tai shogun*" ("barbarian-subduing great general") and "Mikado" was the title of the emperor of Japan. European writers characterized the Mikado as the spiritual emperor and the Shogun as the temporal emperor. In 1867, with the abolition of the feudal system, the Mikado assumed sovereign power and the reign of the Shoguns ceased. The *OED* relates that the "samurai" flourished in Japan "during the continuance of the feudal system, … a class of military retainers of the daimios; sometimes … member[s] of the military caste, whether … samurai or a daimio." "Daimio" was a title conferred on the chief territorial nobles of Japan. The word "bushido" refers to the ethical code imposed on the Samurai; literally, it means "military knight ways."

Japanese delicacies continue to flavour our vocabulary. The year 1880 supplied us with the first citation of "sashimi," a blend of "*sashi*" ("dish") and "*mi*" ("flesh"). The *OED* describes sashimi as a "dish consisting of thin slices of raw fish served with grated radish and ginger and soy sauce." "Sushi" was first used in English in 1893 and "tempura" and "sukiyaki" join the ranks in 1920. The *OED* claims that tempura is an adaptation of the Portuguese "*tempero*" ("seasoning"). "Teriyaki" ("*teri*," "gloss, lustre" and "*yaki*," "roast") is first listed in 1962, and "ramen" in 1972. The *OED* relates that ramen, in Japanese cookery, are the quick cooking Chinese noodles usually served in a broth with strips of meat and pieces of vegetables. A recent *OED* revision marks the addition of "maki zushi," "a dish consisting of sushi and raw vegetables wrapped in a sheet of seaweed."

Since 1863, we've been able to cook in English on a "hibachi," which combines the words "*hi*" ("fire") and "*hachi*" ("bowl, pit").

The Japanese language regales us with far more than food. Joining the lexicon in 1979 was "karaoke," which combines "*kara*" ("empty, void") with "ôke" ("orchestra"). The *OED* says that it is "a form of entertainment, originating in Japan, in which a person sings the vocal line of a popular song to the accompaniment of a pre-recorded backing tape, and the voice is electronically amplified through the loudspeaker system for the audience." "Nintendo" was added to the *OED* in 2003 and we can expect to see "pokémon" there before long.

[Malay]

Malay is a language that few would suspect of contributing many words to English. Malay, known to its speakers as "Bahasa" ("the language") is spoken by close to eighteen million people as a first language and over one hundred million as a second language. It is the national language of Malaysia, and has millions of speakers in Indonesia and hundreds of thousands in Singapore. Malay has a rich history as a lingua franca for many diverse ethnic groups.

The peoples of Malaysia, Singapore, and the Philippines have been seafarers since about 1500 BC. To allow communication between speakers of diverse languages, a trade language developed called "Pasar Malay" ("Market Malay"). Today, the language is known as "Bazaar Malay." It is a pidginized form of Malay. Since late medieval times, Bazaar Malay has been the common trading language for most of the East Indies. Its dominance arose through the port of Malacca (now Melaka) on the southwestern coast of Malaya facing Sumatra. In medieval times, Malacca controlled the straits through which ships had to pass in order to trade. At one time, it may have been the largest port in the world.

The Dutch seized the port in 1641. The British came in the late 18th century through the British East India Company, taking over a group of ports, including Penang and Singapore, that were later called the Straits Settlements. After the Napoleonic Wars they included Malacca. It is not surprising, then, that many of our words from Malay reached English through Portuguese and Dutch.

The first definition of "compound" (in the sense of "enclosed group of buildings") in the *OED* is "the enclosure within which a residence or factory (of Europeans) stands, in India, China, and the East generally." "Compound" comes from the Malay "*kampong*" ("enclosure"). They were first used by the English in the early factories in the Malay Archipelago.

Stockades around the compounds were usually made of locally grown bamboo. This word was originally "*mambu*" in Malay, became "*bambu*" in Portuguese, and "*bamboes*" in Dutch. The Malay word "*bambu*" may have descended from the Indian language Kanarese in the form of "*banwu.*" The bamboo may have been cut with a "kris," a Malay dagger with a wavy blade, or with a "parang," a heavy sheath knife.

The local people were not considered approachable and were thought to "run amok." The first citation of "amok" in the *OED* dates from 1516: "There are some of them who go into the streets, and kill as many as they meet. These are called Amuco." "Amoq" in Malay means "fighting frenziedly."

Given the importance of trade in the area, it is not surprising that some of our words for products derive from Malay. The cloth "gingham" comes from the Malay "*ginggang*," originally an adjective meaning "striped." The "sarong" is the Malay name of the national garment of Malaysia, and derives from the word "*srung.*" Also coming out of this part of the globe is the fabric printing technique "batik." The word "batik," however, comes from Javanese where it means "painted."

The animal kingdom is represented in English in Malay words. "Cockatoo" is rendered in Malay as "*kakatua,*" which became "*kaketoe*" in Dutch. It was probably rendered in English as "cockatoo" because of its resemblance to "cock" ("male bird"). We also get the flightless five-foot "cassowary" from the Malay "*kasuari*" and the name of the lizard-like gecko from the Malay "*gekoe.*" It is said that this word is an imitation of the animal's cry. One of our closest relatives comes from the Malay language, in which it means "man of the woods." I refer to the "orangutan." In Malay, "*orang*" means "man" and "*hutan*" means "forest."

While Malay sometimes gets credited as the source of words whose derivation is really Chinese, some word origins credited to Chinese really deserve to be credited to Malay. A "junk," a flat-bottomed sailing vessel, is thought by some to come from the Chinese "*ch'wan*" ("ship, sailing vessel"). But the Dutch and the Portuguese were established in Java and the Malay Archipelago before they visited China. In Malay, the word for a junk is "*adjong*" and in Javanese it is "*djong.*" Even the word "mandarin," associated with China, is more of a Malay word than a Chinese word. We received the word from the Portuguese "*mandarim*," which in turn came from the Malay and Hindi "*mantri*." Ultimately, the word comes from the Sanskrit "*mantrin*" ("counsellor").

[African]

There are many millions of English speakers in Africa to whom English represents a second or a third language. The recent revision of the *OED* is bringing many Africanisms into our language. For example, from South Africa, we have the words "malombo" (an exorcism rite) and "majat" ("marijuana"). From the Amharic language of Ethiopia, we have absorbed the word "madoqua," the name of a tiny antelope about the size of a hare.

These are words that aren't going to be too familiar to most readers. There are, however, many familiar words of African heritage in our language. Many of them deal with belief systems. The *OED* shows the word "voodoo" to be an adaptation of the African "*vodu*," which, depending on the particular language, means "spirit" or "demon." With the western tendency to associate voodoo with evil, it may surprise some to learn that it is a religion that combines rituals of Catholicism with African religions and magic. Voodoo is derived from African ancestor worship and is practiced throughout the Caribbean and South America as well as in parts of the United States. Also of African origin is the word "zombie," which is associated with voodoo. The *OED* says "zombie" is of West African origin, probably from the Kongo word "*nzambi*" ("god") or "*zumbi*" ("fetish"). It defines "zombie" as "a soulless corpse said to have been revived by witchcraft; formerly the name of a snake-deity in voodoo cults of or deriving from West Africa and Haiti." By the mid 1930s, it had acquired the added sense of a dull, apathetic, or slow-witted person. The first citation of this meaning is drawn from H.L. Mencken's *The American Language*: "Any performer [in a film] not a Caucasian is a zombie."

A word of African origin, "mojo" was made popular by Mike Myers in the film, *Austin Powers: The Spy Who Shagged Me*. It ultimately derives from the West African language Fulani word "*moco'o*" ("medicine man"). The word "*moco*," meaning "witchcraft" or "magic," has been employed in the Black American dialect Gullah, spoken on the islands off the coasts of South Carolina and Georgia. The *OED* defines "mojo" as "magic, the art of casting spells; a charm or amulet used in such spells." In common usage, though, it is usually defined as "libido" or "life force" or, "as the French say, that certain I-don't-know-what," explains Austin Powers.

Also coming from Gullah is the word "juke," as in "jukebox." It most likely derives from the word "*dzug*" in the West African language Wolof, where the word means "to live wickedly." The *OED* relates that the word "juke" has also been used to refer to "a roadhouse or brothel; specifically, a cheap roadside establishment providing food and drinks, and music for dancing." Possibly also from Gullah is the verb "to tote." The word "*tota,*" meaning "to carry," exists in the Kikongo language of the Congo.

The *OED* is uncertain about the origin of the term "mumbo jumbo." There are, however, several accounts pointing to an African etymology. Francis Moore states in his *Travels into the Inland Parts of Africa,* written in 1738, "At Night, I was visited by a Mumbo Jumbo, an Idol, which is among the Mundingoes a kind of cunning Mystery. ... This is a Thing invented by the Men to keep their Wives in awe." In 1799, the explorer Mungo Park describes "a sort of masquerade habit ... which I was told ... belonged to Mumbo Jumbo. This is a strange bugbear ... much employed by the Pagan natives in keeping their women in subjection."

Unfortunately, no one since the 18th century has reported any such deity in any West African tribe. It is possible that "mumbo jumbo" may be a corrupt form of the Kongo word "*nzambi*" ("god"). An alternate theory has the word descending from the Mande group of languages in West Africa. Here, "*mama*" refers to "ancestor" and "*yumbo*" means "pompom-wearer," originally applied to a masked figure worshipped by the Mande people.

Explorers such as Moore and Park dismissed belief in a native god as ignorant superstition. A religious belief in Mumbo Jumbo, a god invented simply to scare the womenfolk, was seen as even more nonsensical. Presumably this gave rise to the modern sense of the term, "complicated and confusing language." The word "bogus" first surfaces at the end of 18th century and originally referred to a counterfeit coin. David Barnhart and Allan Metcalf posit in their book *America in So Many Words* that the word was adopted from the word "*boko*" meaning "deceit" or "fake" in the Hausa language of west-central Africa.

There is no question about the African origin of the word "zebra." The first *OED* citation is from the year 1600: "The Zebra ... of this countrey [Congo] being about the bignes of a mule, is a beast of incomparable swiftnes." Another animal out of Africa is the "gnu." It belongs to the antelope family, but resembles an ox or buffalo in shape. Most etymologists believe that the word is a corruption of the word "*ngu*," used to reference the animal among the San people of southern Africa.

Another animal word of African origin is "chimpanzee," which is recognized in the Bantu languages to be a close relative of man. The *OED* only states that it is "the native name in Angola, in West Africa." Other sources, however, record that it may derive from the Kikongo language where it means "mock man." The first citation of chimpanzee in the *OED* is from 1738 and states, "a most surprizing creature is brought over in the Speaker, just arrived from Carolina, that was taken in a wood at Guinea. She is the Female of the Creature which the Angolans call Chimpanze, or the Mockman."

8

"Native" Contributions

Legend has it that the name "Canada" is based on an inability to communicate. Explorer Jacques Cartier's guides used the Huron-Iroquoian term "*kanata*," meaning "village" or "community," to designate a section of territory occupied by cabins. Cartier took this to be the name of the New Land, hence Canada, "our home and native land," as attested to by the verse in the Canadian national anthem.

Canadian place-names highlight Canada's native heritage. Quebec's Algonquian name means "where the river narrows"; "Ontario" is said to come from the Iroquoian "*kanadario*" ("sparkling or beautiful water"); the name "Manitoba" is believed to come from a Cree or Ojibwa word meaning "strait of the manitou or spirit," and "Saskatchewan" comes from "*kishiska djiwan*" ("rapid current"). Canada's capital, Ottawa, derives its name from the word "*adawe*," which means "to trade." The name was given to the natives who lived along the Ottawa River because they were good hunters and brought quality furs to market. "Toronto" is derived from an Iroquoian word whose meaning is disputed. In the United States, twenty-seven of the American states' names enjoy native derivations. Connecticut derives its name from the Mohican Quinnehtukqut, or "beside the long tidal river" and Minnesota from a Dakota word that means "sky-tinted water."

Many of the earliest North American loan-words come from the Algonquian family of over thirty languages which includes Cree, Mi'kmaq, and Ojibwa. This is not surprising, considering that Algonquian tongues were spoken from North Carolina to Hudson Bay and from the Atlantic to the Mississippi.

Naturally, unfamiliar animals were among the first named items. The word "skunk" comes from the Abenaki word "*segankw*" and means "he who squirts." In *A Dictionary of Canadianisms on Historical Principles*, there is a citation from 1620 of "skunk" as "a small beast like a ferret whose excrement is muske." Some animal names went through a process of word mutation. In 1608, there is a reference to a varmint called a "*rahaugcum*" or "*raugroughcum*." By 1611, it had changed into an "*aracoune*," and in 1624 it became a "*rarowcun*." In 1672, it emerged in its final form, "raccoon." In 1610, Captain John Smith referred to an animal that possessed a "head like a swine, a taile like a rat, and is of the bigness of a cat." It started its spelling journey as an "aposoum," then "opassom," then "opossum," and finally "opossum" by the end of the 17th century. "Caribou" derives from the Mi'kmaq "*khalibu*," which means "pawer" or "scratcher." The word "moose" comes from the Algonquian "*moosu*," where it means "he trims or cuts smooth," an allusion to the proclivity of the moose to strip the lower branches and bark from trees while feeding. Actually, the English language already had the word "elk" for this large animal, but few Englishmen had ever seen the Scandinavian elk. People naturally assume that the woodchuck gets its name from its tendency to "chuck wood." Not so. The word is an anglicization of the Algonquian word for the animal, "*ockqutchaun*."

Plants specific to the Americas are also among the earliest native loan-words into English, and many of these adopted simplified spellings upon their absorption into our language. The vegetable "squash" derives from the rather more complicated "*asqútasquash*," which means "that which is eaten raw," and seems to have originally referred to a melon. Also of native provenance is "succotash," typically a dish in which corn and lima beans are cooked together. This is a derivative of the Algonquian "*msíckquatash*." "Hickory" comes from the word "*powcohoccora*" that the aboriginal people in Virginia applied to the milky liquor they obtained from a common tree in the area. Also coming out of Virginia is the word "pone," corn bread which is rendered in Algonquian as "*poan*" or "*appoans*."

Anthropolgist Edward Sapir said that "Single Algonquin words are like tiny imagist poems." This is because Algonquian, like several other native language groups, is characterized by polysynthesis, the expression of many sentence elements within a single word. Many people assume that a language spoken in a culture that is less advanced technologically will have a simpler structure. Algonquian languages belie this belief. In English, a sentence such as "Peter saw Paul as he was leaving" would be ambiguous. Not so in Plains Cree, an Algonquian language of central Canada, where different verb forms for "see" mark the difference in meaning: "*Peter Paul-wa waapameew, eesipwehteet*" means that Peter is leaving; "*Peter Paul-wa waapameew eesipwehteeyit*" means that Paul is leaving.

Unfortunately, many aboriginal languages spoken in Canada are doomed. In fact, it has been calculated that of the fifty or so native languages in Canada only three—Inuktitut, Ojibwa, and Cree—are expected to survive this century. This is tragic, since culture is intrinsically linked to language and the loss of a language can lead to cultural impoverishment. Echoes of these once vibrant languages, however, will always be heard in the scores of native words that have enriched the English language.

In *Native Tongues*, Charles Berlitz relates that the "llama got its name by mistake. When the Spanish invaders saw the strange animal they asked the Indians, "Cómo se llama?" ("What is it called?"). The Indians, trying to understand what the Spanish were saying, kept repeating the word "llama." The Spanish took their own question as an answer, and dubbed the animal they had been calling "Indian sheep" a "llama." This is a lovely story, except for one minute detail—it's not true. "Llama" was the word for the said animal in the Peruvian language of the Indians. The same myth underlies the origin of the word "kangaroo." Legend has it that Captain James Cook asked an Aborigine the name of the strange hopper and was answered "*Kangaroo*," which supposedly meant "I don't know." "*Kangaroo*," however, was the name the Aborigines had previously applied to the marsupial.

Of course, when one language absorbs a word from another, the word that finally emerges may bear little resemblance to its ancestor. This has occurred with words that Spanish absorbed from indigenous populations in the Americas which were subsequently absorbed into English. For example, the Nahuatl word for "avocado" was "*ahuacatl*." This was the word the Aztecs also applied to a testicle, because the shape of the fruit was similar to a testicle and because of the fruit's supposed aphrodisiac properties. The word "*ahuacatl*" proved to be a mouthful for the Spaniards and they called it "avocado" instead, borrowing the Spanish word for "advocate" or "lawyer."

Sometimes the misinterpretation isn't with the food but with the diner. When Columbus alit in the Lesser Antilles on his second voyage in 1493, he met natives who called themselves "*Carib*" or "*Caniba*," depending on their dialect. Upon hearing the word "*Caniba*," the geographically-challenged Columbus, who believed he was in Asia, asserted, "*Que Caniba no es otra cosa sino la gente de Gran Can*" ("The Caniba are none other than the people of the Great Khan"). Because some of the Caribs were man-eaters, the word "cannibal" in European languages came to refer to a person who eats human flesh. The word may have been also influenced by the Spanish word "*canino,*" which means "canine" or "voracious." The Carib tribe also bequeathed its name to a leaf they smoked: "tobacco." The first *OED* citation for tobacco, from 1588, states: "In these daies the taking-in of the smoke of the Indian herbe called Tabaco, by an instrument formed like a litle ladell, wherby it passeth from the mouth into the hed & stomach, is gretlie taken-up & used in England."

The Spanish were a little more faithful in their rendering of "*cacahuatl,*" the Nahuatl word for "beans of the cocoa tree." This was rendered by the Spanish as "cacao" and by the 18th century it had mutated to "cocoa" in English. Originally it was pronounced with three syllables ("ko-ko-a"), but confusion with the "coco" of coconut (which was sometimes spelled cocoa) led to the current two-syllable pronunciation. The Aztecs also had the word "*xocolatl,*" which the *OED* describes as "an article of food made of equal parts of the seeds of cacao and those of the tree called pochotl." This word was a compound formed from "*xococ*" ("bitter") and "*atl*" ("water"). When this word was adopted by the Spanish in the early 16th century, it was applied to the "drink chocolate"; the sense of solid edible chocolate developed fifty years later.

Many other food terms were rendered fairly accurately on their migration: the Caribbean Indian word "*mahiz*" became "*maize*" in Spanish and "*maïs*" in French; the extinct Haitan Taino tribe bequeathed "*batata,*" which became the Spanish "*patata*" and English "potato;" the Nahuatl "*tomatl*" became the Spanish "*tomate.*" It became "tomato" in English because of the mistaken belief that this was the definitive Spanish ending.

Indigenous cooking techniques have led to some interesting words. The Tainos used a framework of sticks for roasting meat which the Spanish rendered as "*barbacoa.*" This word came to refer to the cooking of the meat itself and came into the English language as "barbecue." This technique of cooking was called "*boucan*" by other tribes in the Caribbean region and this word surfaces in the *OED*'s first definition of "buccaneer"; "One who dries and smokes flesh on a boucan after the manner of the Indians." Pirates often bought dried meat from these boucaniers and eventually the term "boucanier" or "buccaneer" was applied to the pirates.

Usually words that come into English from Spanish are similar to the Spanish word. In many cases the words are identical, including "barracuda," "bonanza," "corral," "papaya," "patio," and "plaza." Occasionally, a Spanish word has been mercilessly mutilated. Captain John Smith reported in 1624 in his *General Historie of Virginia* that "a certain India Bug, called by the Spaniards a cacarootch, the which creeping into Chests they eat and defile with their ill-sented dung." One wonders if Smith, in rendering the first syllable of "cucaracha" as "caca" was influenced by the scatological sense of the word. Within thirty years, the word was being rendered "cockroach" as if the insect was a hybrid of a "cock" ("male rooster") and "roach," a freshwater fish. By the 19th century fastidious Victorians were dispensing with the lurid first syllables and hence a new species of roach was born.

9

Other Englishes

[African English]

If you live in Africa and speak English, you don't necessarily speak African English. The millions of white South Africans are not considered to be speakers of African English; nor are the English-speakers in North African countries such as Morocco and Egypt. The term "African English" is used to describe the way the language is spoken in Black Africa. One hundred million black Africans speak English as either a first or second language.

Some of the English words coming out of Africa give us an inkling of its customs and beliefs. "Lobola" is the custom of handing over cattle to the father of the bride in exchange for his daughter. The word derives from the Nguni *"ukulobola"* ("give a dowry") and the practice is still common for many blacks living in southern Africa. The number of cattle depends on the woman's marriageability; a suitor might have to cough up twenty cows for the daughter of a chief, while the average family could expect a receipt of five bovine creatures. This term has spawned the expression "lobola beast" to describe someone who uses a bride price as a means of exploitation while feigning friendship.

In many West African countries, people will be seen sporting "juju" charms. This word is believed to derive from the French for "toy, plaything." A juju is used as an amulet to provide protection for its wearer. The word is also used to refer to the supernatural or magical power emanating from the charm. In Liberia, the term "jina" is widely applied to refer to any spiritual entity. In Nigeria, the word "obanje" refers to the belief that certain children who die return to the mother's womb and die continuously.

African English also features many intoxicating food and beverage words. While in Central or East Africa you might want to sample "pombe," a drink made by fermentation from many kinds of grain and fruits. It is noted by the *OED* as being first used in 1857, when explorer Richard Burton wrote: "Grain is so abundant that the inhabitants exist almost entirely upon the intoxicating pombe, or holcus-beer." In West Africa, you might want to sample "dika-bread," a vegetable substance somewhat resembling cocoa, prepared from the fruit of a species of mango tree. If you visit Liberia, sample the "dumboy," boiled cassava pounded into a thick viscous dough. An on-line recipe suggests serving it "in a bowl covered with clear water broth or squeezed into a ball and dipped into palm oil soup." A popular dish in Nigeria is spicy "akara balls," which are made with black-eyed peas or white beans. They are sometimes served as a snack or as a dessert with fried bananas or plantains.

There are also distinctive garment words in African English. In Ghana, you might espy someone wearing a colourful "kente," a long garment made from a handwoven banded material, loosely draped around the shoulders and waist. "*Kente*" in the Twi language means "cloth." In most of West Africa, boys wear a piece of cloth fashioned into a simple tunic-like shirt called a "dashiki," which is made of a brightly-coloured embroidered fabric.

African English also features many colourful words and expressions. In East Africa, somebody who overeats isn't referred to as "gluttonous," but "foodious," as noted earlier, and in West Africa, tribal chiefs aren't "enthroned" and "dethroned," but rather "enstooled" and "destooled." Throughout Africa, the term "WaBenzi" (or "MaBenzi") is used in a derisive fashion to describe politicians, businessmen, and others whose success is characterized by their ownership or use of a Mercedes-Benz. Its first documentation in the *OED* is from an 1967 issue of *The Economist*: "Africa is rapidly earning itself the reputation of the world's biggest joke ... the 'Wabenze', the new but already well-known African people whose tribal mark is a ministership and a Mercedes."

There are also many interesting idiomatic usages. In Nigeria, if someone "throws water" at you, they've most likely offered you a bribe; this might be done if you have "long legs," e.g., you wield power and influence. In Nigeria and Cameroon, if you are "in state," you might be "pregnant." In Sierra Leone, "women damage" is the money paid by another man to a husband as compensation for having sex with his wife; in Liberia, an "outside child" is a child known to be born out of wedlock. In East Africa, if a couple asks you to "beat us a picture," they have asked you to take a photograph of them, and if they say of this endeavour, "It's porridge," they have told you that it's "a piece of cake."

African English diverges considerably from what we may call Standard English, but there is no reason that it should not. When asked in 1965 whether it was possible for an African to speak English like a native speaker, Nigerian novelist Chinua Achebe answered, "It is neither necessary nor desirable for him to be able to do so. The price a world language must be prepared to pay is submission to many different kinds of use."

[Australian English]

Once a jolly swagman camped by a billabong,
Under the shade of a coolibah tree,
And he sang and he watched and waited 'til his billy boiled,
"You'll come a-waltzing, Matilda, with me."
    –from the song "Waltzing Matilda"

Welcome to one of the most colourful of the varieties of our language, Australian English. It has a short history, reflecting some two hundred years of European settlement, and an even shorter period of recognition as a national variety, the term "Australian English" being first recorded only in 1940.

To a non-native speaker, Australian English can be one of the most incomprehensible renditions of our mother tongue. The lyrics of the Australian classic "Waltzing Matilda" testify to its obscure vocabulary. It features lines such as "Up rode the squatter," "Up rode the troopers," and "Where's that jolly jumbuck you've got in your tucker-bag?"

A little translation is in order for non-Aussies.

A "swagman" is a hobo who travels into the bush with a "swag," a bundle of personal belongings. Actually, the phrase "waltzing matilda" is somewhat synonymous with "swagman." It originated with German immigrants and "waltzing" is derived from the German "*auf der Walz*," which means "to travel while learning a trade." "Matilda" came to mean "to be kept warm at night" and later referred to the blankets used by soldiers. These blankets were rolled into a swag and tossed over the soldiers' shoulders while marching.

The word "billabong" derives from an Aboriginal name for "bell river." The *OED* cites an example from 1836 and says it derives from the Aboriginal "*billa*" ("water") and "*bang*" ("of uncertain origin"). A "billabong" is a branch or effluent of a river and "*bang*" may derive from an undetermined Aborginal language where it meant "dead." "Coolibah" is another indigenous word and refers to an Australian enamelware pot with a close-fitting lid and wire handle, used for making tea. The *OED* defines "billy" as a "cylindrical container, usually of tin, used over fires in the open."

The term "squatter" has a similar meaning to that in North America, "one who claims land by squatting on it," but it refers to a particular group in Australia. An *OED* citation from 1830 talks about a "clan of people, ... generally emancipated convicts, ... who having obtained a small grant sat themselves down and maintained large flocks, obtained generally in a very nefarious way by having the run of all the surrounding country." The word "trooper" in Australia refers to a "mounted policeman" and "jumbuck" was the name given by Australian and New Zealand Aborigines to "sheep." It originally meant a "white mist preceding a shower" to which a distant flock of sheep was likened by the natives. A "tucker-bag" is a food bag and "tuck" used to refer to the daily food supply of a gold-miner or station-hand.

Many names of animals in Australia, such as "kangaroo," "koala," "wombat," "brumby" (a wild horse), "barramundi" (lungfish), "bunyip" (an amphibious monster), and "kookaburra" (brown kingfisher), are loan words from the Aborigines. But surprisingly, the Aboriginal influence on Australian English is quite limited, for two reasons: first, the white settlers were not interested in the local languages, believing that they were inherently inferior. Secondly, the marked regional variation of Aboriginal languages meant that loan-words were of local currency only.

Although Australian English has added over ten thousand words to the language, few of them have gained an international currency. The largest demand for new words has come from the unique Australian worlds of flora and fauna, and predominant occupations like stock-raising. Because of this, Australianisms are predominantly naming words: single nouns, like "mulga" (acacia), "mullock" (mining refuse), and "muster" (round-up of livestock). We also have several colourful terms, such as "black camp" (an Aboriginal settlement), "black trader" (an Aboriginal employed by the police to track down missing persons), "black velvet" (Aboriginal women regarded as sexual objects), "red-back" (a type of spider), and "red gum" (a eucalyptus).

If there is one hallmark of Australian English, it is its laid-back inform-ality. Thus, the well-known Australian use of "mate" as a form of address between friends or colleagues is meant as a way of putting the addressee at ease and doesn't indicate any disrespect, as the word "mate" often does in Britain. This informality is also displayed by the oft-used ending "-y" or "-ie." We have "rellies," not relatives; "pollies," not politicians; "mozzie," not mosquito; "sandie," for a beach girl; and, of course, "Aussie," for Australian. We also have many shortenings such as "arvo," for afternoon; "derro," for derelict; "smoko," for a smoking break; "reffo," for a refugee, and "garbo," for a garbage collector.

In contrast with North America and Britain, where the pronunciation of words varies greatly with the region, Australian accents are neither region-specific nor class-specific. In Australian English it is also almost impossible to deduce a person's education, regional background, or social status by listening to his or her accent. Visitors to Australia have sometimes lamented that Australian English is more difficult to learn than North American or British English. Some students worry that learning Australian English will mark them as having a peculiar accent.

But what exactly is the Australian accent? Most linguists divide Australian accents into three categories: cultivated Australian, general Australian, and broad Australian. Cultivated is quite similar to BBC English and is spoken by only a small minority of people. The general variety, spoken by over half the population, is a careful but much more relaxed form of speech. The broad dialect (nicknamed "Strine") is the most heavily accented variety and the one outsiders recognize as distinctively Australian. The word "Strine" derives from the tendency of vowels to be distorted and syllables reduced, as in "Strine" itself, where the four syllables of "Australian" are reduced to one. Many of the early white settlers were convicts and their jailers hailed from southeastern England; as a result, broad Australian is similar to the Cockney dialect spoken in some parts of London.

Don't expect to be invited to many exciting parties if someone refers to you as a "wowser," a straight-laced, puritanical person, although this might be preferable to being called a "dag" or "daggy," as the connotation here is of being grungy. There are myriad ways to refer to your quint-essential idiot. In this category, we have the words "dill," "drongo," and "galah." "Galah" is actually the Australian name for the rose-breasted cocka-too. This bird is regarded by some as being noisy and stupid and the *OED* records that in 1944 the word was used with the sense of "simpleton."

A reference to someone as "not the full quid" implies that they are intellectually challenged, as does the expression "kangaroos loose in the top paddock." Also insulting is the term "bludger," as it refers to a lazy person. The term is usually applied to one living on the dole who doesn't try to find work. It's unlikely that you'll be referred to as an "ocker," as the term is generally reserved for an uncultivated, boorish Aussie. The name derives from a character in a series of Australian television sketches.

Australians being a congenial lot, I suppose it's possible you might be occasionally complimented, so don't take umbrage if you're referred to as "dinkum," "grouse," "bonzer," "rootable," "cobber," "spunk," or "tall poppies." "Dinkum" means true or genuine; "grouse," great or very good; "bonzer," attractive or very good; "spunk" refers to a good-looking person of either sex; "rootable" means one is sexually attractive; a "cobber" is a friend; and "tall poppies" designates successful people.

Other oft-referenced items Down Under are "norks." The first citation to the word in the *OED* is the following 1962 entry from Criena Rohan's *The Delinquents:* "Hello, honey, that sweater—one deep breath and your norks will be in my soup." "Norks" (as you may have surmised) is Australian slang for "breasts." The word apparently derives from Norco Co-operative, a butter manufacturer in New South Wales.

Australians also seem to possess a veritable stream of terms for vomiting. We have the terms "liquid laugh," "technicolour rainbow" (sometimes rendered as "technicolour yawn"), and "big spit." Some other off-colour terms include "brown-eyed mullet," for a turd espied floating in the ocean; "crack a fat," meaning to achieve an erection; and "pillow biter" for a homosexual man. If you are a neophyte surfer, you might be referenced as a "shark biscuit."

Increasingly, English is becoming a less formal language. Rather than diminishing the language, this informality has led to greater inventiveness. So, in a sense, what is called Standard English is becoming more similar to Australian English, which has always been inventive in describing our ever-changing world.

[Canadian English]

At present the *Canadian Oxford Dictionary* (*COD*) contains words such as "arborite," "bangbelly," "download" (in the sense of one level of government passing a cost to another level), "garburator," "poutine," and "smoked meat" that are absent from the pages of the *OED*. The *COD* Second Edition of 2004 added the word "schlockey," a form of hockey played by school children with cut-off hockey sticks and a hockey puck on a 4x8-foot sheet of plywood. The *OED* will eventually add all these words to its lexicon.

I must say that Canada's contribution to the vocabulary of English is not always fully appreciated. A number of years ago I heard a commentator on National Public Radio in the United States declare that his country was "the first pluralistic society in the history of the world." Concurrently, I was reviewing a book on neologisms that listed words on the cusp of being accepted by American dictionaries, such as "digerati," "flatliner," and "generation X." One of the breakthrough entries was a word that seems ancient to us Canadians, "multiculturalism." It had taken the so-called "first pluralistic society in the world" a quarter-century to accept a word that has been a mainstay in Canada since the 1960s.

While the North American Free Trade Agreement (NAFTA) negotiations were being hammered out between Canadian and American delegates, Canada had declared that Canadian culture was "not on the table." A sardonic American involved in negotiations asked a CBC reporter what she thought the difference was between Canada and yoghurt, and then informed her that "Yoghurt has a living culture."

So we Canadians don't have culture, eh? Have a gander at this, Yank:

> It was a classy party. The *beerslinger* posted a sign warning that "*suckhole hosers* with *Molson muscles, rubbies* and *shit-disturbers* are not welcome." No sirree. Folks were drinking *bloody Caesars* and *brown cows* at the *booze can*. Heck, even *Gravol* was free.

The italicized entries may not be in your average home dictionary, as they are all true-north Canadianisms. They find a home, however, in the *COD*. A little translation is in order for non-partying or non-Canadian elements. "Beerslinger" is an informal term for a bartender; a "hoser" is a lout; "rubby" refers to a derelict alcoholic known to include rubbing alcohol in his cocktail; "Molson muscle" is a term for a beer-belly; "brown cow" and "bloody Caesar" are names for cocktails; and a "booze can" is an illegal bar, usually in someone's home. Canada now joins Australia, New Zealand, and South Africa in having its own indigenous Oxford dictionary. And you thought that Canadian English consisted of no more than the word eh, eh?

If a Canadian spends any amount of time with Americans, she or will be informed rather quickly about some of his quaint Canadianisms. When an American is nauseous, or headachy, she won't reach for Gravol or ASA but for Dramamine and Apirin. Javex, Varsol, and garburator may be Canadian household items but an American will not know what these terms mean and will reference them as chlorine bleach, mineral spirits, and garbage disposal unit, respectively.

Lots of words and phrases that Canadians use every day are not to be found in most dictionaries. I discovered this recently when I entered a manuscript through my computer's spell-check. Indispensible words, such as "anglophone" ("English-speaking person") and "francophone" ("French-speaking person") do not exist as legitimate words in the database. Canadians are prone to using expressions such as "March break," "seat sale," and "book off" (work) without realizing that less northerly English speakers don't necessarily know what we are talking about. In some cases, words that we use may not be known outside of a particular province. Take the expression "two-and-a-half" to refer to an apartment with a combined living room/bedroom, kitchen, and bathroom. This is strictly a Quebec English usage. Then again, I don't think too many Quebecers are familiar with the Newfoundland "bangbelly." It is a pudding, cake, or pancake consisting of a dumpling-like mixture that is fried, baked, or stewed.

Dining in Canada can also be a unique experience. You will not find too many of these words in non-Canadian dictionaries: "poutine" (french fries topped with cheese curds and gravy); "tourtière" (French-Canadian meat pie consisting especially of ground pork and spices); "all-dressed" (pizza with all the trimmings); "steamie" (steamed hot dog); and "smoked meat" (cured beef similar to pastrami but more heavily smoked). COD even had the gastronomical sense to have an entry for "Montreal bagel," which is defined as "a type of bagel, originally made in Montreal, which is lighter, thinner, and sweeter than other kinds of bagels."

The preface to COD states that it is the fruit of "five years of work by five Canadian lexicographers examining almost twenty million words of Canadian text held in databases representing over eight thousand different Canadian publications—fiction and non-fiction books, newspapers, magazines, even theatre programs, grocery store flyers and Canadian Tire catalogues." Of particular note in the Second Edition of the dictionary are pages 1432-33, which feature the following excretory headwords: "shit-faced," "shit for brains," "shithead," "shitkicker," "shitless," and "shitload."

Incidentally, in the United States, a "shit-disturber" is more likely to be called a "shit-stirrer."

Many common words acquire a Canadian flavour in the *COD*. Take the word "shovel." In the *OED*, it is defined as a device to remove "quantities of earth, grain, coal or other loose material." In Canada, when we think of shoveling, the definitive object we think about is snow, and a shovel is defined as a "spadelike tool for shifting quantities of snow, coal, earth, etc." The verb "to shovel" is defined as "to clear (an area) of snow, etc. using a shovel (shoveled the driveway)."

Even some of the most innocuous words can attain a Canadian flavour. Definition #5 of the word "across" in *COD* reads as follows: "Cdn (Prince Edward Island) in or to Nova Scotia or New Brunswick (go across, come from across)." Similarly, one of the definitions of "away" is "Cdn (Newfoundland and Maritimes) in a place other than the speaker's home province or Atlantic Canada in general (they're from away)."

And of course, the *COD* also features countless hockey terms, such as "dump the gloves" and "dump and chase," that pepper our lexicon. One could be excused for believing that Canadian politics is a form of cryptohockey. The following headlines have graced Canadian newspapers since the 1990s: "Joe Clark [the former Prime Minister of Canada] Must Now Stickhandle Route to New Federalism"; "Mr. Klein's [a premier of Alberta] Entire Government Is Based on the Spin-a-rama"; "Joe Ghiz [the former Premier of Prince Edward Island] Hangs up His Skates Because He Is Feel-ing too Old and Tired for the Game of Politics;" "Prime Minister Paul Martin's Minority Could Yet Crumble Over the Scandal Left Behind by His Predecessor Unless He Can Successfully Stickhandle Past the Gomery Commission" and "But the Politicians Who Want to Ban VLTs Always Skate around the Real Issue." By the way, the word "puck" appears 102 times and "hockey" 398 times in the Second Edition of the *Canadian Oxford Dictionary*.

Dining in Canada involves eating many distinctively named foods. For example, the word "*achigan*" is unique to Quebec French, denoting two species of bass. It was borrowed early into Canadian English and French from Cree and Ojibwa, where "*achigan*" meant "struggler, splasher, fighter." "*Pâté chinois*" ("shepherd's pie") has an eastern etymology, but not as far east as you would think. Many 19th century Québécois migrated to the northeastern United States to work in mills. Some settled in the town of China, Maine, and brought back a recipe for shepherd's pie that they called "*pâté chinois.*" "Pie" actually figures in an etymological dispute over the origins of "*cipaille,*" a layered meat pie. English etymologists favour the theory that "cipaille" is a bastardization of the English phrase "sea pie." French etymologists are more likely to endorse an origin from the Latin "*caepa*" ("onion") because both the dish and the bulb are multi-layered.

"Poutine," the bane of cardiologists, stems ultimately from the English word "pudding." "Le pudding" is used France in 1678 to refer to "pudding steamed in a cloth bag." In the dialect of Nice, pudding became "*la poutina,*" but it referred to a melange of fried sardines and anchovies in lemon oil. The most recent reincarnation of poutine occurred in Quebec in 1957. Legend has it that truck driver Eddy Lainesse had a culinary epiphany at Fernand and Germaine Lachance's café in Warwick, Quebec. Lainesse suggested mixing the cheese curds with fries. *Et voilà!* The gravy was not beef gravy at first, but Germaine Lachance's special recipe of brown sugar, ketchup, and a drop or two of Worchestershire sauce.

In *Your Mother's Tongue*, Stephen Burgen wrote that "anti-clericalism is an act of defiance by a God-fearing peasantry against a clergy that sancti-fied poverty and the status quo that sustained it." There's a large amount of anti-clerical humour in all dialects of French and some of this humour is reflected in the names given to foods. In Acadian French, the little dessert pastries that resemble cinnamon rolls are referred to as "*pets de soeurs*" ("nuns' farts"). Sometimes they are called "*bourriques de soeurs*" ("nuns' belly buttons"), or, in more genteel society, "*rondelles*" ("slices") or "*hiron-delles*" ("swallows"). The epitome of sacrilegious dining, however, is prob-ably to be found in the Quebec treat "*oreilles de crisses.*" These are little slices of salt pork grilled or fried, but literally the terms translates as "Christ's ears," so-called from the way the little slices curl up when grilled.

From coast to coast, Canada features some appetizing (and not so appetizing) morsels. A traditional Sunday morning breakfast in New-foundland is "fish and brewis." "Brewis" is hard bread, also known as "ship's biscuits," soaked in water and cooked with salt cod, and often served with scrunchins, which are cubes of fatback pork fried golden brown and tossed over the brewis as a garnish or mixed right in with the cod and bread. Prince Edward Island's famed Malpeque oysters grow to juicy maturity in the waters of Malpeque Bay. "Malpeque" is an Acadian French rendering of "*Mak Paak,*" "big bay," from Mi'kmaq, the language of the island's earliest named residents. The Nova Scotia town, lake, and river of Shubenacadie take their name from a French and English rendering of a Mi'kmaq phrase signifying the presence of "*sequbbun*" ("groundnuts").

Our First Nations have also bequeathed us food words in the Prairies. "Saskatoonberry" comes from the Cree word "*mi-sakwato-min*" ("tree-of many-branches berries"). The recipe for the soupy stew "rubbaboo" was to chop up pemmican (pounded, dried buffalo meat) and toss it into boiling water. "Rubbaboo" apparently comes from the Algonquin word "*ruhiggan*," which means "beat meat."

For dessert we offer B.C. "soapolaillie." These are soapberries whisked with water until they froth up and with other wild berries like wild raspberry added, along with sugar, to sweeten the naturally slightly bitter soapberry.

For those with gamier palates, may I recommend beaver tail, in which the tail is cut off and blistered over a fire until the skin loosens. After the skin is removed, the tail flesh is boiled in a large pot of beans. Or, if you prefer, you can dine on moose muffle soup. Bill Casselman, in *Canadian Food Words*, informs us that a moose muffle is the "nose and the pendulous, overhanging upper lip … eaten boiled, baked or fried as a delicacy."

Compared to Americans, Canadians tend towards hedging and understatement. Whereas something might be described as "awesome" in the U.S.A., in Canada it's more likely to be designated as "not bad," or if one is given to Canadian hyperbole, as "O.K." Ask an American how he or she's doing and the answer is liable to be "Great;" the Canadian is liable to answer, "Surviving."

And who other than a Canadian can express so many thoughts with a two-lettered interjection? In the book *Canajun, Eh?* Mark Orkin translates:

> "I'm walking down the street, eh? (Like this, see?) I had a few beers en I was feeling priddy good, eh? (You know how it is.) When all of a sudden I saw this big guy, eh? (Ya see.) He musta weighed all of 220 pounds, eh? (Believe me.) I could see him a long ways off en he was a real big guy, eh? (I'm not fooling.) I'm minding my own business, eh? (You can bet I was.)"

Perhaps the ubiquitous Canadian usage of "eh" is a way of asking for reassuring feedback, as if to say, "Do you?" or "Don't you think so?" As such, don't you think it's the most civilized way to end a sentence, eh?

[Caribbean English]

Indian English, a subdivision of Asian English, is spoken by over forty million people; Philippines English, a subdivision of East Asian English, has almost forty million speakers; and Nigerian English, a subdivision of African English, has approximately forty-five million speakers. On the other hand, Caribbean English, while scattered over one million square miles of sea, has no more than six million speakers, and even that is when we combine native speakers with second-language speakers. Yet Caribbean English is considered to be one of the eight main varieties.

David Crystal points out in *The Cambridge Encyclopedia of the English Language* that "the label 'Caribbean English' is used with more geographical than linguistic accuracy to refer to its distinguishing properties." It isn't even clear if the term refers only to English or if it includes creolized English. So why is Caribbean English recognized as a distinct variety?

To understand why, we must briefly look at the origins of Caribbean English. The slave traders who commenced kidnapping Africans in the 17th century made a point of bringing people of different language backgrounds together on the ships, in order to make it harder for rebellion to develop on board. The result was the growth of several pidgin, or simplified, forms of communication, and in particular a pidgin between the slaves and the sailors, many of whom spoke English. Once these ships alit in the Caribbean, pidgin continued to serve as a major means of communication between the black population and the slaveholders and among the blacks themselves. When the slaves started having children, pidgin gradually began to be used as a mother tongue, producing the first black Creole speech in the region. Creolized forms of Dutch, French, Portuguese, and Spanish were also being developed in the Caribbean, and some of these interacted with the creolized English, leading to the incredible diversity of Caribbean English. So when we use the term Caribbean English, we are including a broad range that includes varieties of British and American English spoken with regional accents to the creolized forms of English.

Any discussion of creoles entails an attempt to explain the differences between pidgins and creoles. Generally speaking, a pidgin is a system of communication that develops among people who do not share a common language and who need to communicate with each other. One obvious situation that would militate this need is trade between people speaking mutually incomprehensible languages. Another was the plight suffered when Africans who spoke mutually incomprehensible languages were kidnapped and placed on slave ships with each other. Pidgin languages are rudimentary and have limited vocabularies, reduced grammatical structure, and a narrow range of functions compared to the languages from which they derive. They are languages of necessity and are used in situations where communication otherwise would not be feasible. A creole is a pidgin that has become the mother tongue of a community. The simple structure of the pidgin remains, but since the creole is a mother tongue it must be capable of expressing the complete range of experience and as a result the vocabulary expands and usually more elaborate syntactical systems evolve.

Naturally, creoles developed among the children born of the slaves working on American plantations. Creoles will also arise, within a multi-lingual community, when the use of the pidgin becomes so common that it serves as a lingua franca for that community, including being used by people who might share a separate mother tongue. Under these circumstances the children of the people who are using the pidgin start to hear the language in their homes leading some of them to use the pidgin as one of their first languages, thereby creating a creole.

Aside from the creolized forms, there exists in the Caribbean a variety of Standard English, chiefly British or American, which is spoken by an educated minority. But although Standard English is the official language in most Caribbean countries, it is in fact spoken by only a small proportion of the nationals of each island state. While some learn Standard English as a mother tongue, a much larger number acquire it in school as a second language.

Some terms, such as "calypso," "dreadlocks," "guppy," and "Rasta" have entered Standard English, but most of the distinctive Caribbean English is regionally restricted. Each island has a wide range of distinctive lexical terms, often relating to the local plants and animals or the local culture. Only 20 per cent of the vocabulary used in Jamaica, the Bahamas, and Trinidad is shared by each of the other island communities.

One will find some colourful terms whose use may be restricted to one or more islands. If you "catspraddle" in Trinidad and Barbados, you've fallen headlong and are sprawled on the ground either because of your clumsiness or because you've been struck a blow. "Spraddle" is a dialect word for "sprawl" and "catspraddle" is perhaps referencing a cat's ability to fall from a height and land on its outstretched paws. A "duppy," in the Bahamas, Barbados, and Jamaica, can refer to a harmful invisible supernatural presence believed to be raised from the dead. In Jamaica, the term "mampala" is used to refer to an effeminate man, and by extension, to a homosexual. It derives from the American Spanish "*mampolin*," which referred to a common rooster, as opposed to a fighting rooster. Also in Jamaica, an incapable, worthless, or stupid person might be called a "nyamps," derived from an undetermined African language. On some islands, a flatterer might "sweet-mouth" you instead of "sweet-talk" you. If he or she doesn't, you might get "touchous," not "touchy."

Many common words take on distinct meanings in Caribbean English. In Trinidad, to "fatigue" someone is to tease or taunt them with a mixture of half-truths and imaginative fabrications, and "to lime" can mean "to loiter." On many islands, "miserable" can mean "mischievious" and "spar" can refer to a friend. In Jamaica and Belize, the word "jacket" is sometimes used to refer to the progeny of a married woman and a man who is not her husband.

There are, however, some unifying aspects in Caribbean English. There is a distinctive rhythm of speech, so that a word such as "Jamaica" tends to be pronounced with three equal beats by a speaker of Caribbean English. There is also a proclivity for certain grammatical forms to be used, such as the tendency for "would" to replace "will" as in, "I would go there tomorrow" and the passive use of "get," as in "It get break." Also, questions tend to be marked by intonation rather than by inversion, as in "You going home?" instead of "Are you going home?"

So while Caribbean English might not enjoy a great number of speakers, its diversity and its distinct history qualify it as one of the eight recognized varieties of our language.

[Indian English]

According to the *Oxford Companion to the English Language*, "an estimated thirty million people (4 per cent of the population) regularly use English, making India the third largest English-speaking country in the world." According to a 1995 analysis, India possessed thirty-seven million speakers of English as a second language and approximately 320,000 first-language speakers. It is fair to assume that ten years hence, this figure has increased dramatically. English also serves an important function in India, as the country possesses almost a thousand languages, but only Hindi and English can be understood throughout the country.

British journalist and satirist Malcolm Muggeridge once quipped that the last Englishman would be an Indian, and this is borne out by many words and expressions that have become archaic in England that one still hears in India. I visited a website that said, "Now we can all enjoy a few glasses of jolly good Indian wine without spoiling our reputations or the delicious food." People will use expressions such as "out of station chappies" and call the trunk of a car a "dicky," terms that are all but extinct in England. Certain words that are used have actually been declared "obsolete" by the *OED*, such as "condole" ("to offer condolences") and "prepone" (the opposite of postpone), are quite common in India.

Indian English grammar can sometimes be perplexing to outsiders. The order of words can vary from the norms of Standard English. In Indian English it is acceptable to say, "What you would like to buy?" or to say, "It is the nature's way. Office is closed today," or to state, "My all friends are waiting." Also acceptable are verbal constructions such as "He is having many books," "I am understanding it," and "The street is full of litters." The present perfect is used often instead of the simple past so someone might say, "I have brought the book yesterday." Certain verbs might be employed differently. For example, one doesn't "obtain" permission; rather, one "takes" permission.

Many terms in Indian English are different from Standard English yet still understandable to outsiders. An "issueless" marriage is childless; a "body bath" is an ordinary bath; a "head bath" is hair washing; "batch-mate" refers to a classmate; and "allotee" refers to a person allotted property. One could probably surmise that "cousin-brother" and "cousin-sister" refer respectively to male and female cousins and that a "Himalayan blunder" is a grave mistake and no mere molehill-sized gaffe. Once you know that the suffix "wallah" denotes a profession, it becomes obvious that a "police-wala" is a policeman or policewoman. If involved in riot control, chances are the "policewala" will be carrying a "lathi," a stick two to five feet long which may be lead-weighted. This might be useful against a "goonda" ("hooligan").

Of course, many other usages are not as obvious. An "uncle" or "auntie" can refer to any male or female adult. Just as "intermarriage" indicates marriage of persons of different religions or castes, "interdine" means to eat with someone outside your religion or caste. If a father is looking for a "mutual alliance," he is probably trying to find spouses for both his son and his daughter. In southern India a "military hotel" refers to a restaurant where non-vegetarian food is served, and a "by-two coffee" refers to a restaurant order by two customers each asking for a half cup of coffee. "Swadeshi" cloth refers to homemade cloth and a "swadeshi hotel" refers to a "native restaurant."

Some terms must simply be learned. "Tiffin" refers to a light midday meal, "tiffin box" to a lunch-box, and a "tiffin room" to a "snack shop." A "dining leaf" is a banana leaf used to serve food and a "kaccha road" is a dirt road. A "grameen" bank refers to a village bank designed to aid the less affluent and a "panchayat" to a village council.

Indian English is fond of hyphenated words. In this category, we have "mixy-grinder" ("food blender"). The terms "anti-people," "ace-defector," and "Eve-teasing" refer to sexual harassment. A billboard in Calcutta announces "Eve-teasing an offence: Roadside Romeos, have you encountered them? Have you been harassed?" It lists many forms of harassment and advises women, "Do not overlook such things. It will only embolden them." An editoral in 2004 in the newspaper *The Hindu* stated that "Eve-Teasing is a rampant social evil. It is all pervasive—beaches, roads, cinema halls, buses and sadly even in educational institutions. When Eve-teasing persists even inside educational institutions, one can obviously infer that even the educated youth don't necessarily desist from indulging in this uncouth behaviour."

For the last half century, Indians have been exacting a modicum of revenge on the legacy of the British Raj by reinventing English. In 1947, Indian writer Raja Rao was one of the early advocates of a distinct Indian style of English: "We cannot write like the English. We should not. … Our method of expression therefore has to be a dialect which will some day prove to be as distinctive and colourful as the Irish or the American. Time alone will justify it." Seeing that India in the last two decades has supplied two Man Booker Prize winners, Salman Rushdie and Arundhati Roy, for the best novel in any Commonwealth country, I think it is fair to say that time has spoken. A character in Hanif Kureishi's 1995 novel *The Black Album* affirms, "They gave us the language but it is only we who know how to use it."

[Irish English]

While the Irish Gaelic language has a special claim on the Irish people, it is unlikely that the language will ever again be widely used as a vernacular. It has become stylish in Ireland to sprinkle one's English with Gaelic elements and many people will say "*Garda*" instead of "Police," "*An lár*" instead of "city centre," and "*An Post*" instead of "Postal Service," but an Irish linguist with whom I communicate speculates that only 5 to 10 per cent of the Irish population are capable of maintaining a reasonable conversation in Irish. But everybody in Ireland speaks "Irish," in the sense that the English used in Ireland is heavily affected by elements from the Irish language. The word "boxty" is a kind of bread made of grated raw potatoes and flour. It derives from the Irish "*bacstaidh*" ("mashed potatoes"). This traditional dish is celebrated in the rhyme, "Boxty on the griddle, boxty in the pan, if you can't make boxty, you'll never get your man." Another colourful word of Irish descent is "bosthoon," which derives from "*bastun*" ("whip made of greenrods" or "softer senseless person"). Other words with pejorative senses have Irish roots. A "spalpeen" refers to a "common worker" or "rascal." The *OED* says it may derive from the Irish "*spailpin*," but says the origin is uncertain. A "culchie" is a city dweller's not totally complementary term for a country denizen. It derives from an Irish county called "Coilte Mach." The term "gombeen" is listed in the *OED* with the meaning "money-lender," coming from the Irish "*gaimbin*." It is also one of the multitude of words the Irish use to describe an idiot. Not listed in the *OED* is the term "kitter," which references a left-handed or clumsy person; it derives from the Irish "*citeog*" ("left-handed side").

It is the synthesis of Gaelic and English elements that provides the specialness of Irish speech. *The Story of English* by McCrum, Cram, and MacNeil supplies us with a wonderful example of a couple courting by the church: 'Tis an aise to the gate they to be married," which translates into Standard English as "Did you know that for years before they were married, they used to meet at the wooden gate?" Ultimately, this would be a direct translation of the Irish "*Is mór an suaimhneas don gheata iad a bheith pósta*," which literally means "It's a relief to the gate that they're married." Another loan translation is the Irish-English expression "at all," which comes from the Irish "*ar chor ar bith*."

The Irishness of Irish English transcends vocabulary. The stress on syllables varies from Standard English, so that a word such as "discipline" is rendered as "disci'pline" rather than "di'scipline" and "architecture" is rendered as "archite'cture." Particularly in working-class Irish-English speech, words such as "leave" and "tea" sound like "lave" and "tay," and "cold" and "old" emerge as "cowl" and "owl." In the south of Ireland words such as "thin" and "then" are pronounced more like "tin" and "den." The grammar of Irish English also is marked by distinctions. In Irish, the expression "*An maith leat e*" means "Do you like it?" so the word "and," often pronounced "an," commences many a question. Also, because Irish does not possess words for "yes" and "no," many people tend to answer questions without them, for example, "Will you go to church with me?"/ "I will," and "Is this beer yours?"/"It is not." The closest Irish comes to "yes" are the words "*maise*" ("indeed") and "*cinnte*" ("sure"). Also seen as distinctively Irish is the use of the word "after." An expression such as "I'm after doing that" does not refer to some future action, but means that the task has been completed.

The Irish Gaelic influence on meanings can be seen in words such as "destroy" and "drowned." For example, a person might say, "He has his son destroyed with presents" because the Irish equivalent "*mill*" means "to spoil" and the verb "*báite*" means "drowned" as well as "drenched." One can also get confused about the meanings of words. Someone who says that she has "No mass in these things now" is not a lapsed Catholic losing her religion. Here, "mass" means "respect" or "faith," deriving from the Irish "*meas*." Someone who is "backward" may be "shy," "glow" can mean "noise," and "to doubt" can mean to "believe strongly."

Also, Irish English is categorized by distinctive idioms such as "He'd put the day astray on you" ("He'd waste your day"); "You'll knock a while out of it" ("It'll last you for a while"); and "She's the rest of yourself" ("She's related to you"). If someone tells you that they are "as weak as salmon in a sandbox," they've related the fact that they're hungry.

[New Zealand English]

If you ask someone to name a word in English of Maori origin, chances are they'll be able to come up with "kiwi." Hence, I was somewhat surprised to discover that the *OED* lists 292 words of Maori origin.

Linguist David Crystal describes New Zealand English as the "dark horse of World English regional dialectology." In classifications of the different varieties of English, the language spoken in New Zealand is usually grouped with Australian English and most people think it is identical to Australian English in all salient respects. New Zealanders, like Canadians, tend to define themselves negatively, explaining to outsiders that they aren't Australians, just like Canadians explain that we're not Americans.

In fact, New Zealand English is quite different from Australian English. What really distinguishes it is the way it has been affected by Maori culture. The Maoris represent one-eighth of the population of New Zealand and so it is no surprise that New Zealand English has absorbed many Maori words.

Legend has it that the Maoris, travelling in a group of seven canoes, left a Polynesian port around the turn of the first millennium and when they finally hit land, they called their new home Aotearoa, "Land of the long white cloud." In 1642, the area was "discovered" by Dutch explorer Abel Tasman, who at first called the islands "Staten Landt" and then opted for the name "Nieuw Zeeland," after the province of Zeeland in Holland. James Cook made three voyages to the islands in 1769, and in 1840 Britain formally annexed the territory.

The only English word of Maori origin that predates Cook's arrival is "mako," a term for a blue-white shark, first recorded in 1727. The year 1773 is marked by a citation for the word "wahine," a term for a Maori woman. The word "taboo" is shown as being adopted from the Tongan "*tabu*," but the near form "*tapu*" is the general Polynesian and Maori form. Cook himself is credited with the first citation of this word in his 1777 *Voyage to the Pacific*: "Not one of them would sit down, or eat a bit of any thing. ... On expressing my surprize at this, they were all *taboo*, as they said; which word has a very comprehensive meaning; but, in general, signifies that a thing is forbidden."

Many of the words of Maori origin in the *OED* give us a brief glimpse at Maori customs and beliefs. "Mana" can refer to power in general, but it also has the religious sense of an impersonal supernatural power that objects and people can possess and pass on to others. A "karakia" is a chanted prayer designed to focus the mind and unite people in purpose. Traditional Maori prayer invokes the creation and reminds people to live in harmony with nature. The *OED* defines a "tangi" as a lamentation or a dirge but this doesn't really explain its significance. It embraces the funeral rites accorded a person before the body is finally interred. The Maori believe that the body of the deceased person should not be left on its own at any stage after death. Hence people will gather to take the body from the funeral parlour to a place where it will lie in the company of people until burial. The word "Reinga" in Maori means "place of leaping." In Maori lore, it refers to the place where departed spirits make their way into the next world.

On a less lugubrious note, we have the word "hongi," which refers to the pressing (but not rubbing) of noses together as a form of salutation. "Haka" refers to a Maori ceremonial dance accompanied by chanting. During wartime, it is a threat dance designed to cause one's enemies to retreat before a battle. When performed without weapons, it is meant to welcome and entertain visitors. A version of this dance is performed by the New Zealand All Blacks rugby team before all their matches.

In some cases, the words in New Zealand English that are of Maori descent are corrupted versions of the original words. The "*piripiri*" in Maori is a shrubby plant used as tea and medicine and is usually rendered in English as "biddy-biddy." The "*kokopu*," a type of fish, has mutated into English as "cockabully." The Maoris have used some English words and given them back to English in altered form. The *OED* shows entries for "plurry" and "pykorry," respectively corruptions of "bloody" and "by golly."

Although the *OED* lists many words of Maori origin, I suspect that future editions will include still others. Not included at present in the *OED* are "*aiga*," a system of extended family; "*hikoi*," a type of protest march; and "*rahui*," a sign warning against trespassing. A school website in New Zealand that I visited states that "A rahui can be placed on an area by the mana authority, power of an elder, tribe, hapu (sub-tribe) or family and stays until it is lifted."

It is time to bid you "*kia ora*," the most common Maori greeting. "*Kia*" means "Let it/there be" and "*ora*" means "health/good fortune/all the good things of life," so the phrase goes beyond our "thanks" or "goodbye" to express a wish of good fortune and all other good things to the recipient.

[Pakistani English]
The countries that comprise South Asia have a combined population of 1.4 billion. English is the major language linking this region to the rest of the world; in some countries it is the only language that is understood by people who speak many diverse tongues. This situation is largely an

outcome of British commercial, educational, missionary, and imperial influences since the 17th century.

In Pakistan, English has enjoyed co-official status with Urdu since independence in 1947, but the constitution of 1959 and successive amendments have recognized Urdu as pre-eminent. In 1981, a study recommended that "Urdu should be the only medium of instruction at the school level, with no exception," but added that Arabic and English should be introduced as additional languages from age eleven.

At higher levels of education, English has an enhanced value and is the dominant language in technological and business spheres. It also enjoys a major media presence and is an important language of communication among a national elite. Estimates show that approximately 2 per cent of the population is bilingual in English, representing almost 2,000,000 English speakers.

Pakistani English can take some acclimatization for the uninitiated. For example, I spotted the following headlines in some Pakistani on-line newspapers: "London *Eveninger* Tenders Apology to Sikhs"; "Pakistan Minister Attends *Moot* in Amman"; "Tribal *Jirga* Leaves for North Wazirstan." An "eveninger" is an "evening newspaper"; a "moot" is a meeting, and a "jirga" is an assembly or council. Some other stories I perused featured unfamiliar words such as *"biradari"* ("clan"), *"dacoit"* ("robber"), *"kabbadi"* (a team sport that meshes wrestling and rugby), *"kachchi abadi"* ("shantytown"), *"namaz"* ("prayer"), and *"wadera"* (a Sindhi landlord).

One also encounters words that have become obsolete in British English, such as "stepney" ("spare wheel"), "dickey" ("trunk of a car"), "conveyance" ("means of transportation"), "teachress" (female teacher), and the use of "tantamount" as a verb meaning "becoming equivalent." The last *OED* example of usage of this word as a verb is from 1716: "Tantamounting in a more reform'd perfection to the different religious orders." A *Pakistan Times* editorial asserted that "we cannot support the demand of a confederation as it tantamounts to the dismemberment of the country." There are also some distinctive words for quantities such as "crore" ("ten million"), "lakh" ("one hundred thousand"), and "maund" (a denomination of weight). Sometimes, unfamiliar nouns will perform double duty as verbs. "Challan" means "citation" and "chowkidar" means "watchman." In the journal *English Today*, linguist Robert Baumgardner cites two examples of this verbification process from Pakistani newspapers:

"The resident magistrate raided the premises ... and *challaned* fifteen of them for various offences," and "Wrought iron gates that lock in the night are *chowkidared* during the day."

Another tendency in Pakistani English is to combine Urdu words with English words or suffixes. Here we have "biradarism" ("favouring one's clan or family"), "goondaism" ("thuggery"), "wheat-atta" ("wheaten flour"), and "gheraoed" ("surrounded by protestors"). Cigarettes can be bought in a "paan-shop" ("spice store") and one can eat a sandwich on "double-roti" (two pieces of bread).

One can often deduce the meaning of terms in Pakistani English from the context. For example, "opticals" are "glasses;" "patchwork" means "repair," and "gadget" means "appliance." On the other hand, familiar English words may have different meanings. A "hotel" can also refer to a "restaurant" and if someone tells you that he can't meet you because he has a "preoccupation," he means that he has a "previous engagement."

Phrasing will often be slightly different from Standard English. Universities employ "academicians," not "academics," who might gobble "toast pieces" instead of "pieces of toast" in the cafeteria. The use of prepositions also may vary from English norms. One doesn't "cope" with a problem, one "copes up," and one "stresses on" and "disposes off" rather than "stresses" and "disposes of." One "participates" an activity rather than "participating in" the activity. In Pakistan an "affectee" is "a person affected" and a "shiftee" is a person shifted from one area to another. You can also be "de-notified" and "de-shaped" and if you fly you can "airline" or "aircraft." If you suffer from kleptomania, Pakistani English can provide you with a "lift" as it doesn't restrict you to being a "shoplifter." Other "lifting" possibilities include "auto-rickshaw lifting," "motorcycle lifting," and even "baby-lifting."

We also see semantic extension in the political realm, an example of which is the expression "horse-trading." A story in *International News* a couple of years ago proclaimed that "Until yesterday horse-trading was an evil that needed to be fought." Obviously, the paper was declaiming more than mutual back-scratching. In Pakistani politics, parties hell-bent on stealing the majority in parliament will target elected members of the opposition parties and offer a bribe to entice someone to defect to their parties. It's called "horse trading" because the process has been likened to the buying or trading of an animal.

[Philippines English]

Armed *Barangay* Self-defense Units to Help Stem Kidnappings.

"The National Coconut Coordinating Council, an *aggrupation* of coalitions and organizations of coconut farmers, submitted a draft ..."

"The justice department said 38 per cent of *plantilla* positions nationwide for prosecutors are still vacant."

The above are either headlines or news items I culled from the *Manila Times* and the italicized words highlight the distinctive English vocabulary spoken in the Philippines. English is one of the two official languages there. The other was previously referred to as "Tagalog," but since the Philippines became independent in 1946, the indigenous language has been called "Pilipino" (in local pronunciation) and "Filipino" (in Spanish and English). This was done to associate the name with the whole nation because traditionally the Tagalog language had been associated almost exclusively with the Manila area and Luzon.

Explorer Ferdinand Magellan claimed the islands for Spain in 1521 and the name "Philipines" honoured the then monarch Philip II. Spanish control lasted until 1898, when the islands were ceded to the United States at the Treaty of Paris. English-language education began in 1901 with the arrival of 540 American teachers. English became the language of education and as its use expanded it became indigenized through the inclusion of vocabulary from local languages and the adaptation of English words to describe local conditions and to satisfy local needs.

After independence the stature of English diminished and in 1974 an education policy was instituted dictating that English be taught only at the primary school level. At higher levels of education, however, English is far more dominant. Close to the forty million people, representing more than half the population of the Philippines, are fluent or semi-fluent in English.

Some of the distinctive words connected to Philippine English, such as the italicized words in the quotations above, tell us something about the history of the islands. The "barangay" was established by President Ferdinand Marcos in the 1970s as a kinship-based political unit, and the word is often used in the sense of "neighbourhood." The original barangays were the large boats used by Malay settlers who arrived thousands of years ago. These newcomers settled in scattered communities that were also called "barangays." The word derives from Malay and refers to the number of people that can fit into a large boat. Other Philippine English words connected to society have been adopted from Spanish, such as the above-mentioned "aggrupation," adopted from the Spanish "*agrupoación.*" The word "plantilla" is used in many contexts to mean "staff," "pattern," or "faculty assignments"; it derives from the Spanish "*plantilla*" ("staff").

Naturally, many words in Philippine English derive from Tagalog. In this category we have "carabao," from "*kalabow*" ("a water buffalo"); "sampaloc," from "*sampalok*" (the fruit of the tamarind); and "kundiman," a love song. A word from Tagalog that has tunneled its way into Standard English is "boondock" (from "*bundok,*" "mountain"). The word was originally adopted into American English in the 1940s with the sense of "rough country;" now it is usually rendered as "the boondocks" and refers to a provincial, unsophisticated locale otherwise known as "the sticks."

Phillipine English can be quite creative in arranging linguistic elements. A thief becomes a "holder-upper" who might "carnap" your vehicle. If the miscreant is more upscale, she might be charged with "estafa," not fraud. Some other interesting combined elements are "cope up," a combination of "keep up" and "cope"; "jeepney," a blend of "jeep" and "jitney bus"; and "captain ball," the captain of a sports team, or more generally, to a person in charge of a situation.

There is no shortage of Spanish adoptions in Philippine English. Examples include "asalto" ("surprise party"), "merienda" (a light meal in the afternoon), "bienvenida" ("welcome party"), "querida" ("mistress" or "sweetheart") and "oppositor" ("opponent").

Food words also abound. The term "viand," an English word that is now rarely used in Standard English, refers to a dish served to accompany rice in a Philippino meal. Several food items including fish, pork, and eggplant may be cooked "inihaw" ("grilled"). "Bagoong" is a paste made from fish or shrimp that is salted or fermented for several weeks. There are all sort of "pancit" (rice-noodle dishes), including "pancit palabok," described by one source as "a merienda of noodles bathed with shrimp gravy sauce and garnished with sliced boiled pork, flaked smoked fish, ground chicharon or pork crackling, sliced hard boiled egg, and chopped green spring onion." "Adobo" is a national dish comprised of braised chicken or pork. Some distinctive fruits are "kalamansi," a citrus fruit halfway between an orange and a lime, and "ampalaya," a bitter melon.

The high level of fluency in English does not please everyone in the Philippines. Some argue that English is the language of colonialism and of a privileged elite and that the use of English in the Philippines should be curtailed. English-language advocates argue that English is a natural means of expression and promote its use because as an international language it protects them against insularity and allows them access to the whole world.

[Scottish English]

Recently, I visited Edinburgh Castle, originally built as a stone fortress in the 9th century. I searched throughout the grounds for an inscription in Scots Gaelic, a language that has been spoken in Scotland since the 4th century A.D. After an hour of fruitless scouring, I solicited the aid of an official and she directed me to the only inscription in Gaelic on the whole castle grounds. In the Scottish National War Memorial there is the following six-word Gaelic inscription: "*Mo dhùthaich, m'onoir is mo dhia*" ("My country, my honour, and my God").

By 500 A.D., a tribe of people from Northern Ireland called the Scoti had began to settle in Argyle on the west coast of what is now Scotland. These immigrants spoke Gaelic, a Celtic language, and they called their new kingdom Dalriada. By 900, the Scoti of Dalriada had absorbed and integrated the original Pictish inhabitants and formed the kingdom of Alba north of the rivers Forth and Clyde. Shortly afterwards, the British kingdom of Strathclyde became part of the kingdom of Alba. About 970, the Northumbrian kingdom became part of the kingdom of Alba, creating the borders of modern Scotland that have hardly changed since.

But Scots Gaelic is not the only indigenous language in Scotland. There is also Scots, which was originally a northern variety of English brought by the Angles who landed in Northumbia and occupied the southeastern parts of Scotland in the seventh century. Throughout this period, the Northumbrians spoke and wrote Anglian, the northernmost variety of Old English. Eventually, northern Northumbria became southeast Scotland, while the rest became part of northeast England.

Even if Gaelic becomes extinct in Scotland, it will always have an influence on English. For example, "cairn" comes from "*carn*" ("heap of stones"); "slogan," from "*sluagh ghairm*" ("host-cry"); and "whisky" from "*uisgebeatha*" ("water of life"). Originally, the Gaelic "*clan*" referred to the children of a family. It was absorbed into English with the sense of a family group led by a chief and having a common name. Recently, this connotation has been reabsorbed back into Gaelic Scots. Gaelic has also contributed elements to the English which has been used locally in Scotland, in terms such as "finnock" ("sea trout") and "larach" ("site").

In his *Encyclopedia of the English Language* David Crystal asserts that "Of all the varieties of English which have developed within the British Isles, there are none more distinctive or more divergent from Standard English than some of those associated with Scotland." I was therefore surprised while on my sojourn in Edinburgh to find that the language in Scottish newspapers I perused didn't diverge at all from that in the newspapers I have read in England.

In an article entitled "Is Scots a Language?" in the journal *English Today*, linguist A.J. Aitken states that in Scotland, "Government, the law, the pulpit, the press, the broadcasting media, education of all levels, officialdom of all kinds, use Standard English—distinguished only by a Scottish accent and in a special vocabulary for certain professions." For example, the Scottish legal system doesn't use the terms "libel" or "slander," but only recognizes "defamation." Likewise, "arson" is referred to in Scottish English as "fire raising" and "manslaughter" as "culplable homicide." In fact, outside of certain specialized publications, the public use of Scots tends to be restricted to literature and folklore, to a few television and radio programs about local issues and to jocular contexts, such as comic strips.

Officially, Scottish English, often referred to as "Scots," doesn't exist. It is not the subject of any official policy like Welsh or Scottish Gaelic, and there are no Scottish as a Second Language courses offered to foreigners. It is best to think of Scots as a private language that the majority of Scottish people mix on an everyday basis with English.

While linguists might squabble about whether Scots is a separate language or a dialect of English, there can be no doubt that it has many distinct elements. There are words that are recognized as having a Scottish provenance, such as "clan," "glengarry," "haggis," "kilt," "loch," and "wee." Many words, however, that enjoy a Scottish origin have been in our language for so long that we forget their Scottish roots. These include "caddie," "collie," "croon," "eerie," "forbear," "glamour," "gumption," "pony," "raid," "scone," "uncanny," and "weird," among many others.

Many words used in Scottish English are rarely used outside of Scotland. A "cleuch" is a "gorge" and a "brae" is a "swoop of a hill." If someone calls you "braw," be complimented, as your good looks have been referenced; if you're called "glaikit," take umbrage, because it has been suggested that you're "foolish" or "stupid-looking." If someone gives you directions to his "but and ben outwith" of Glasgow, he has related that he resides outside of the city in a two-room cottage ("but" refers to the outer room and "ben" to the inner room). If they ask you not to be "fashed" about coming to the "Hogmanay" party, they've asked you not to bother about going to the New Year's party. Both these terms derive from French. "Fash" derives from the French "*fâcher*" and "Hogmanay" ("New Year's Eve") is from the Old French "*aguiillaneuf*" ("New Year's gift").

Many common words have different meanings in Scottish English. "To jag" can mean "to prick," "to sort" can mean "to mend," "to uplift" means "to collect," and "to big" means "to build." A "close" refers to an entry passage in a tenement building, and if someone admires your large "lugs," 'tis your ears they're talking about.

Some words thought to be restricted to use in Scotland are also used in the north of England such as "bairn" ("child"), "dwam" (stupor), "blether" (talk nonsense), "haffet" (cheek), and even the term "Hogmanay." On the other hand, the use of "pinkie" to refer to the little finger is rare in England, but common in Scotland and North America. While "stane" is used to replace "stone" in Northern England as well as Scotland, the use of "chuckiestane" (pebble) is unique to Scotland.

There are also several grammatical distinctions to Scottish English. There is the guttural consonant "ch," found in words such as "loch" or the dismissive interjection "ach." There are also distinctive verb forms. "Go/went/gone" becomes gae/gaed/gan(e)" and "give/gave/given" transforms into "gie/gied/gien." Pluralization also might vary from Standard English, as "eyes" becomes "een" and "shoes" becomes "shuin." Nouns of measure remain unchanged in the plural, so "two miles" becomes "twa mile" and "five pounds" is rendered as "five pun."

The Scots often use language in a jocular fashion. In the *Oxford Companion to the English Language*, Tom McArthur refers to their "willingness to move ... from a more Scots to a more English way of speaking, employing differences in pronunciation, grammar, vocabulary, and idiom which add to the nuances of communication. The middle classes may parade Scots, especially Gutter Scots, proudly, humorously, snobbishly, or patronizingly, according to the inclination and circumstance." The working class, for their part, will often mock someone they consider affected or too English by using "anglified" speech.

I will leave you with one of my favourite Scottish toasts: "Lang mey yer lum reek," which literally means "Long may your chimney smoke," but which translates as "Live long and happily."

[Singlish]

When Being *Kiasu* Isn't All Bad
It Was *Shiok*, Man!
Makan by the Bay
–Headlines from the *Electric New Paper*

According to the *Oxford Companion to the English Language* (*OCEL*) our mother tongue is available in some quite exotic sounding flavours such as Hapa-Haole (Hawaii Pidgin English) and Bislama (a variety of Melanesian pidgin). With the exception of Japlish (a mixture of Japanese and English), the -lishes such as Spanglish (Spanish and English), Chinglish (Chinese and English), and Hinglish (Hindi and English) are excluded from the *OCEL* because the -lish suffix denotes a sub-standard variety. For this reason, some academics refer to the English spoken in Singapore as Singapore English and not as Singlish even though this term is employed by virtually everyone in Singapore.

The indecipherable headlines above come from a Singaporean newspaper and some translation is required for the italicized Singlish terms. "*Kiasu*" is a Hokkien Chinese term that means "fear of losing to others" or "losing face." "*Shiok*" is a Malay-derived adjective that literally means "delicious" but is often used to mean "great." "*Makan*" means "to eat" or "food" in Malay and it is used in the same sense in Malaysian English and Singlish.

Singlish is a creole formed from elements of English, Malay, Cantonese, and Hokkien Chinese and is looked at askance by Singaporean government officials. In 1999, Senior Minister Lee Kuan Yew wrote that "we are learning English so that we can understand the world and the world can understand us. It is therefore important to speak and understand Standard English." In 2001 the government launched a "Speak Good English" movement in an attempt to persuade the bulk of the population converse in Standard English as opposed to Singlish.

On the fifth anniversary of this campaign in 2005, Prime Minister Lee Hsien Loong expressed embarrassment upon meeting "the son of an Australian friend of mine. The young man had just graduated from a very good school in Melbourne. I asked him if he had any schoolmates from Singapore. He said there were a few. He then commented that they spoke a strange type of English among themselves. It sounded like English, but he could not make out the meaning at all. In fact, they were speaking Singlish! My friend observed that they did not seem to distinguish between 'no' and 'not.' It took me a little while to think of an example in Singlish— 'Money No Enough!'"

Perhaps this attempt at language engineering is admirable but I suspect that efforts such as this to eliminate local forms of English are doomed because it is the nature of widely spoken languages to fragment into dialects.

In addition, dialects such as Singlish represent a strong unifying force across ethnic boundaries, levels of income, and levels of education. These dialects reflect the needs, personality, and linguistic roots of the indigenous area. In Singapore, people are proud that they speak a distinctive no-nonsense form of English. Singlish phrases or sentences tend be more concise than in Standard English and natives see this pithiness as fitting the needs and the temperament of their fast-paced society.

While Singlish may help define an individual, it can be a handicap if a Singlish speaker wants to converse with Standard English speakers. I believe the solution lies in speakers of dialects such as Singlish becoming bilingual. Linguist David Crystal says,

> In a future where there are many national Englishes ... people would still have their dialects for use within their own country, but when the need came to communicate with people from other countries they would slip into "World Spoken Standard English." So, a multinational company might decide to hold a conference at which representatives from each of its countries would be present. The reps from Calcutta, sharing a cab on their way to the conference, would be conversing in informal Indian English. The reps from Lagos ... would be talking Nigerian English. The reps from Los Angeles would be using informal

American English. Any one of these groups, overhearing any other, might well find the conversation difficult to follow. But when all meet at the conference table, there would be no problem; everyone would be using "World Standard Spoken English."

[South African English]

Afrikaans (the African form of the Dutch language) is the first language of the majority of South African whites, many of whom also speak English fluently. One estimate shows that over 45 per cent of the total South African population speaks the country's second official language, English. In *The Oxford Guide to World English*, Tom McArthur asserts that "as a lingua franca, English is used with varying proficiency by millions of blacks whose mother tongues are not English, and is commonly mixed with them in terms of pronunciation, grammar, vocabulary, and rhetoric."

Certain English words are generally associated with South Africa. Observe "aardvark," "apartheid," "Boer," "eland," "kraal," "rand," and "veld." Most people would be surprised to discover that major dictionaries feature many other words and terms that originated in South Africa, some of which are widely used. The word "commando" was originally used in South Africa to refer to military expeditions of the Portuguese or the Dutch Boers; it comes from the Portuguese "*commando*" ("party commanded"). The original sense of "trek" in South Africa was the voyage by ox-wagon between two stopping points. The inaugural "concentration camp" was instituted by Lord Kitchener during the Boer War (1899-1902) and referred (non-euphemistically) to camps where non-combatants of a district were concentrated.

There are, however, many terms used in South African English whose use rarely transcends the country. For example, there are words to describe those who tend to the human spirit, such as "predikant" and "dominee," both of which can reference a minister of the Dutch Protestant Church in South Africa. A "sangoma" is a witch doctor, usually a woman, who claims supernatural powers of divination and healing. There are even distinctive words for potable spirits such as "tshwala" (from Nguni), which is brewed with malted grain or maize, and "mampoer," which is brandy distilled from peaches or other soft fruit. This concoction may have been named after the Sotho chief Mampuru, who was executed after a rebellion in the Transvaal in 1883. Distinctive food terms include "boerwors" ("farmer's sausage"); "braalvleis" (a term for a barbecue which literally means "grilled meat"); "sosaties" ("curried kebabs"); "putu" (a type of porridge); "potjiekos" (a stew made in a three-legged pot over an open fire); and the Anglo-Indian "brinjal" ("eggplant"). There are distinctive adjectives, such as "lekker" ("pleasant" or "excellent"), "larney" ("smart" or "pretentious"), "verkrampte" ("narrow-minded"), and "staunch" ("burly" or "strong").

As one would expect, there are local words to describe the landscape. Aside from "veld," which refers to "open country," there is "kloof," which refers to a ravine or gorge between two mountains, and "klip," which can refer to a rock or a diamond. From African languages, there is the word "karoo," which refers to barren semi-desert tracts, and "donga," which is a gully formed by the action of water. Sometimes a common word will take on a particular sense in the South African landscape. "Drift" is used to refer to the passage of a river and "land" itself can refer to a cultivated piece of ground, usually fenced. When you leave the countryside and move into the cities, don't forget to obey "robots," e.g., "traffic lights."

If you are visiting South Africa, you might hear strange words to describe everyday things: "gogga" instead of "insects," "dorp" (a small town), and "bioscope," a term for "cinema" used by older South Africans. Someone might say, "The chemist (pharmacist) gave me a muti for my 'babelaas.'" The word "muti" is used in a colloquial sense to refer to a remedy. It comes from the Zulu "*umuthi*" ("tree," "plant," or "medicine") and originally designated a medicinal charm used especially by witch doctors. "Babelaas" is a South African English term for a hangover that derives from the Zulu "*babalazi*" ("dulling after-effects of carousal").

Not surprisingly, the grammar of South African English is influenced by Afrikaans. For instance many South African English speakers say, "Is it?" to mean "Really?" or "Is that so?" The expression comes from the Afrikaans "*Is dit?*" Prepositions are also affected by Afrikaans, so one is likely to say, "She is by the school," not "She is at the school," and "She's not here on the moment," instead of "She's not here at the moment." Certain Afrikaans expressions have been assimilated, so one would probably say, "The village boasts with beautiful vineyards," rather than "The village boasts beautiful vineyards." Idiomatic usage might also be confusing. Don't be heartened if someone tells you, "You have two chances," because this is equivalent to the Standard English "You have no chance at all."

10

Changes to the English Language

One of the great strengths of the English language is the acceptance by its speakers that our language never stands still and that it should not be encumbered by any academy that would seek to dictate its use. The vocabulary of English is swelling and the *OED* will be adding innumerable words to our language during the next decade.

Alas, because language is in a constant state of flux, a lexicographer's work is never done. The Second Edition of the *OED*, published in 1989 in twenty volumes, is a classic example. According to *The Oxford Companion to the English Language*, this edition has "21,728 pages and contains some 290,500 main entries, within which there are a further 157,000 combinations and derivatives in bold type (all defined) and a further 169,000 phrases and undefined combinations in bold italic type, totaling 615,500 word forms." Commencing in March 2000, that edition of the *OED*, plus three volumes of additions, became available on-line through the medium of the World Wide Web.

Present plans are to incorporate at least a thousand new and revised entries each quarter.

The *OED* is also undertaking the first complete revision of its print version in its history and hopes to have the work completed by the year 2010. Thus, a hundred and twenty years after the first editor, James Augustus Murray, launched an "Appeal for Words for the *Oxford English Dictionary*," John Simpson, the present chief editor, invited "readers to contribute to the development of the *Dictionary* by adding to our record of English throughout the world. Everyone can play a part in recording the history of the language and in helping to enhance the *Oxford English Dictionary*." Simpson stated, "There is no longer one English—there are many Englishes. Words are flooding into the language from all corners of the world. Only a dictionary the size of the *OED* can adequately capture the true richness of the English language throughout its history, and the developments in world English." The present *OED* will expand to a rather unwieldy total of over forty tomes upon the completion of the next edition in 2010.

One reason so many words are being added is because of the lexicographic advancements in some of the "other" Englishes.

What's the difference between a "motormouth" and a "megamouth"? What's the difference between "moby" in the U.S.A. and "moby" in Britain? Thanks to additions to the *OED*, we can know the answers to these conundrums. A "motormouth" is a person who talks fast or incessantly, whereas a "megamouth" is a plankton-eating shark. "Moby" (adj.) in the U.S.A. means "impressive or large" (as in Moby Dick) and "moby" (n.) in Britain is a colloquial term for a mobile phone.

Right from the first revisions I was struck by the amazing details the *OED* now supplies. Not only has the quantity of words mushroomed, but the *OED* keeps finding new facts about existing words. Take the word "mafia." It used to be believed that "mafia" was a long-established name for a Sicilian institution, and the word "mafioso" simply denoted a member of the society. New research, however, reveals that "mafioso" derives from the old Sicilian word "*mafiusu,*" borrowed from a Spanish or Arabic word meaning "scoundrel." "Mafia" was inferred from "mafioso" and was born only around 1860, after which it migrated into English. The revised entry for the word "macaroni" revealed that in the 16th century, it meant a dumpling, closer to what we now know as "gnocchi." The *OED* explains how the word, which originally was the name of a mere cereal gruel, extended its meaning and is now used to refer to a penguin, an 18th-century dandy, a coin, a form of verse ("macaronic"), "nonsense" in Australian English, a wood-carving tool, and a small violin. The previous entry for "mumzer" stated, "A bastard. Also in extended uses as a term of abuse." The revised entry is far more thorough: "A person conceived in a forbidden sexual union, especially as defined by rabbinical tradition. Also in extended uses as a term of abuse or familiarity."

In the first thousand new and revised entries from "M" to "MAH" alone, there are many representatives from our well-traveled English language. Here's a brief sampling: "macoute" (from Haitian Tonton Macoute), "thug" (from the Caribbean), "Machiguenga" (a "Peruvian American-Indian people"), and "mack" ("smooth talker, with the aim of seduction," from the U.S.A.). Canadian English is well represented, with terms such as "Macgillivray's warbler" ("wood warbler"), "macoun" ("dessert apple"), "mackinaw" ("cargo boat formerly used on the Great

Lakes"), and "MPP" (an abbreviation for "Member of Provincial Parliament").

I was struck by the number of words that are rendered as verbs. We are now able "to mentor," "to memo," and "to modem," and if we are theatrical, we can "miscue," i.e., "miss or mistake a cue." Other verbs include "Mickey Mouse," defined as "To waste time in trivial or irrelevant activity," and "McDonaldize," defined as "To make [something] resemble the McDonald's restaurant chain or its food." It does not take long for words to become verbified. The *OED*'s first citation of "motormouth" as a noun is from 1963; by 1983 it is shown as being used as a verb. McDonald's is also the inspiration for the new term "McJob," defined as "an unstimulating, low-paid job with few prospects, especially one created by the expansion of the service sector."

What has 600,000 words and describes 750,000 terms used in English over the past thousand years? Answer: *The Oxford English Dictionary* (online version) launched on March 14, 2000 at www.oed.com. Although still in its nascent stage, this revision could double the length of the *OED*, taking the number of words and phrases from 640,000 to 1.3 million.

The year 2000 saw approximately four thousand new and revised entries but thereafter the annual output has been increased to meet the scheduled completion date of 2010. Leading the way in the inaugural edition are one thousand revised and updated words from "M" to "MAH." John Simpson, chief editor the *OED*, said the revision began with the letter "M" because "We wanted to start the revision at a point halfway through the dictionary where the style was largely consistent, and to return to the earlier, less consistent areas later."

The *OED Online* offers many ingenious search possibilities. Let's say I want to check what expressions King Harold might have used in the months before an arrow pierced his eye at Hastings. Entering the year "1066" in the "quotations date" box reveals an entry for the word "wardwite," which was "a fine paid to the lord by a tenant who failed to provide a man to perform castle-guard." The term "infangthief" referred to "jurisdiction over a thief apprehended within the manor … to which the privilege was attached."

A feature called "proximity search" is another useful tool. For example, if you want to know if there is a word for the action of grinding your teeth, the proximity search helps uncover the term "bruxism." If you want to check "edible mushrooms," a simple search may not find all references to "edible mushrooms" in the dictionary because in some entries this exact form of the words may not occur. In this instance, a "proximity search" would do the trick. Crossword afficianados will be aided by a search function that seeks words with only some letter clues. Enter f**k and discover possibilities such as "faik," "a fold in anything; as a ply in a garment (Jamaican)"; "fank," "a sheep-cot or pen"; "feck" ("to steal"), and "firetruck."

Not surprisingly, Shakespeare is the most quoted individual in the *OED*, but let's say we're looking for sayings from lesser lights such as John Lennon or Dr. Seuss. No problem. The headword "bullshit" has the following citation: 1970, J. Wenner's *Lennon Remembers*: "He is a bullshitter. But he has made us credible with intellectuals." The first citation of "nerd," from 1950, is, naturally enough, from its progenitor Dr. Seuss, who wrote in *If I Ran the Zoo*, "And then, just to show them, I'll sail to Ka-troo. And Bring Back an It-Kutch, a Preep and a Proo, a Nerkle, Nerd and a Seersucker, too!"

Simpson believes that the print edition of the *OED Online* will be the definitive tome of tomorrow: "I am sure it will be the version that most people will consult. A dictionary of perhaps forty volumes will be rather unwieldy, but the present [twenty-six-volume] hardback has many fans and the [*Online*] *OED* in traditional book form is by no means out of the question."

I asked chief *OED* philologist Edmund Weiner whether all the Englishes that now exist would be treated equally in the Third Edition. Weiner admits that for those areas where there is a long-established community of L1 English (people to whom English is their first language) and the *OED* has a "fairly long tradition of lexicography research" it is "easier to cover them well by drawing on that tradition. As research begins to take place in the other communities and a bank of data about the varieties spoken there builds up, we will be able to cover them better, but inevitably it will take time." Weiner is being modest, for the process of covering the "other communities" better in the *OED* is well under way.

Weiner gave me an inkling of the future by saying the inclusion of the Nigerian English "*ogi*" ("cornmeal"), the Philippine English "*barangay*" ("village"), and the Indian English "*mandir*" ("temple") were all slated to be added.

One can see in checking the new entries, however, that a veritable feast awaits us. From around the globe, new dishes are being served up in the pages of the *OED*. Let's look at the new culinary terms starting with the letter "M." We have "maque choux" (a "Cajun dish of creamed corn and other vegetables, especially peppers and tomatoes"). Although its etymology is uncertain, the *OED* hypothesizes that it comes from the term "mock cabbage," "*choux*" being the French word for "cabbage." "Pasanda" is a north Indian dish consisting of slices of meat, traditionally lamb or kid, beaten thin and cooked in a rich sauce made with tomatoes, yogurt, cream, and often almonds. "Payasam" is an an Indian dessert consisting of rice or vermicelli, boiled in milk or coconut milk, flavoured with cardamon, and often containing ground nuts.

From Japanese, we are offered "maki zushi," which is a "dish consisting of sushi and raw vegetables wrapped in a dish of seaweed," and "mizutaki," a dish which is comprised of of chopped meat, usually chicken on the bone, which is boiled with vegetables or tofu, in water or a thin broth lightly seasoned with kombu seaweed stock or fish stock. In a Japanese restaurant, the term "omakase" refers to a menu choice in which the chef decides what food the customer receives. It derives from the verb "*makaseru*" ("to trust").

"*Mee krob*" in Thai means "to be crisp." In English, it refers to a Thai dish consisting of crisp fried noodles served with prawns and pork or chicken. If one's taste for fish is still not sated, one can sample "maomao" from Maori, a "blue-skinned marine food fish" found in New Zealand and Australian waters, or "medaka," a type of small Asian freshwater fish. The word blends the Japanese "*me*" ("eye") with "*daka*" ("high"). "Mariscos" derives from Spanish or Portuguese and is a type of shellfish served as a dish which was first referred to in Hemingway's 1932 novel *Death in the Afternoon*.

If one is seeking a hearty dish, try "merguez," which is a spicy sausage made of beef and lamb and coloured with red peppers. It was originally made in the French colonies of North Africa but later became popular in France and elsewhere. The word derives from the Maghribi Arabic "*mergaz*."

Although I remember it appearing on Chinese food menus when I was a boy, only recently has "moo goo gai pan" appeared in the *OED*. For the uninitiated, this is a dish consisting of stir-fried strips of chicken with mushrooms and assorted vegetables. For those who prefer non-Asian fare, we have "metagee," which in Guyana refers to a thick stew containing vegetables, fish, salted meat, and coconut milk, and having a distinctive grey colour, or "mostaccioli," a variety of pasta in the shape of short, hollow tubes with diagonally cut ends. For hardy folk with gamier palates, "mooseburger" (Bullwinkle's least favourite food) has just been added to the *OED*.

We also find some new animals in the revisions. A "marl" is a small light-coloured bandicoot with a striped rump. The word derives from the Aboriginal Nyungar language spoken in the Perth-Albany area. From Maori, we find the "matuku," a slate-grey egret found on the coasts of Australasia and southeastern Asia. South Africa provides the "maanhaar," a cross of a jackal and an aardvark, and the "nagapie," which refers to any of the various bushbabies found in these parts. The word is an adaptation of the South African Dutch *nachtaapje* ("night ape"). From Ethiopia, we have the "madoqua," a small antelope the size of a hare; the word is an adaptation of the Amharic *medaqqua.* From Japanese we have the "medaka," a freshwater fish found in paddy fields, and Sinhalese provides us with the "malkoha," a large non-parasitic cuckoo.

The *OED* is also listing heretofore unnamed groups of people. Under "M" we find the "Machiguenga," members of an Arawak people inhabiting Peru, and the "Mapuche," members of any of the Araucanian Indian nations of central Chile and Argentina. "Machiguenga" is American Spanish for "people" and "Mapuche" is an Araucanian blend of *mapu* ("land") and *che* ("people"). Moving north, in the Americas we are introduced to the "Mangoak," North American Indians who inhabited parts of North Carolina in the 16th and 17th centuries and spoke an Iroquoian language. The word comes from the Iroquois word for enemy, *menkwew.* The Phillipines offers some new names, such as the "Manobo" (literally "river people"), who are a group of "proto-Malay people on Mindanao," and the "Mangyan," who are members of "distinct ethnic groups inhabiting upland Mindoro, an island in the Philippines." And let us not forget the "Magar," members of one of the tribes of Western Nepal, of Mongol origin and noted for their prowess in fighting, nor the "Mansi," members of an "Ugrian people of West Siberia, formerly called Vogul," nor the "Mwera," who speak a Bantu language and inhabit an area of south-eastern Tanzania.

* * *

As of December 15, 2005, revision and addition of words from "M" to "philandering" had been completed. To demonstrate the dynamic influences exerted by the "other Englishes," here are some morsels from various parts of the globe that help you become multilingual within your own language.

India and South Asia have brought us new terms to describe groups of people. "Mahar" refers to a member of a caste of western India, whose duties include village watchman and public messenger. A "Mishmi" is a member of a hill-dwelling people inhabiting Arunachal Pradesh and parts of Assam in northeastern India. "Nuristani" refers to a member of a people inhabiting part of the Hindu Kush area of northeastern Afghanistan, or to the languages spoken by these people. "Mleccha" in ancient India designated a non-Aryan or person of an outcaste race. In modern times, the word is used to refer not only to a foreigner but to someone who does not conform to conventional Hindu beliefs and practices.

There are also many new words to portray types of individuals. We have "mahant," a religious superior; "mahout," an elephant-driver; "neta," a term for a leader; and "mukhiya," which is often reserved in parts of India and Nepal to refer to the headman or chief of a village. I mentioned earlier that an "allottee" is someone who is allotted property. Indian English now has added an antithesis to this in the word "oustee," which refers to someone who has been forced to leave their home due to the development of property. Both a "matranee" and a "mazdoor" would be lacking in status. The former designates a female servant engaged to perform the most menial tasks in a household, and the latter describes an unskilled labourer in both India and Pakistan. In South Asia, a "nazar" is a present or tribute given by a social inferior to a superior. The term derives from the word "*nazr*," which in Urdu, Persian, and Arabic means "undertaking" or "offering."

Many words in Indian English reveal elements of Hindu culture. In India, "mardana" refers to that part of the house reserved for men to which women are not usually permitted. "Marma" is a word borrowed from Sanskrit and refers to any of the number of sensitive points in the body through which energy is believed to flow. "Nyaya" also derives from Sanskrit where it means "universal rule"; and it is one of the six systems of orthodox Hindu philosophy. "Mala," in Hinduism and Sikhism, refers to a necklace or a string of prayer beads, and in Indian jewellery-making "minakari," from Urdu or Persian, refers to the decoration of gold with intricate enamel-work designs. "Mundu," in parts of southern India, refers to a large piece of cloth worn wrapped around the waist and, when worn by men, frequently features the lower back edge pulled up between the legs and tucked into the waistband. The word "mela" has two meanings, both ultimately descending from Sanskrit; it can refer to a religious fair or festival among Hindus. In Sanskrit this word means "assembly"; it also has the meaning of a musical scale around which a raga is formed. "Onam" is a Hindu harvest festival celebrated in August and September in Kerala in southwestern India.

East Asia is also providing many new English words that tell us much about cultural activities. "Miai" denotes the initial formal meeting of the prospective partners in a Japanese arranged marriage. This meeting may have been arranged by a "nakodo," who is the person who acts as intermediary in arranging the introduction of the prospective parties and who assists in negotiations. This word derives from the Japanese "naka" ("middle").

Do not confuse "manga" with "Nanga." The former refers to a Japanese genre of cartoons and comic books, drawn in a meticulously detailed style, usually featuring characters with distinctive large, staring eyes, while the latter is an expressive style of Japanese painting which developed from the Chinese Southern school and was practiced in Japan during the 18th and 19th centuries. "Mingei" designates Japanese folk art and handicraft, especially as represented by functional everyday objects; "monogatari" is a story or narrative, and in particular a romantic legend; "onnagata" is a man who plays female roles in Japanese kabuki theatre—the term blends "onna" ("woman") with "gata" ("shape"); and "nogaku" refers to a Japanese Noh drama, which is a masked drama with dance, mime, and song.

An "otaku" is the Japanese equivalent of a computer "geek" and literally means "your house, home." In Japan, the word sometimes connotes obsession bordering on psycopathy, but increasingly the term, particularly outside of Japan, is worn as a badge of honour. A June 7, 2005 article in the *Washington Post* entitled "In Tokyo, a Ghetto of Geeks" stated, "It was just another night out with the pocket-protector crowd in Tokyo's neon-splashed Akihabara district, where 'costume cafés' are the latest of hundreds of new businesses catering to Japan's *otaku*, or nerds." Perhaps an otaku will have a "meishi," a small card printed with the bearer's name, address, telephone number, etc. The word is a compound of the Japanese words "*mei*" ("name") and "*shi*" ("calling card").

China has provided some new words such as "Mahayana." The word blends the Sanskrit words "*maha*" ("great") and "*yana*" ("vehicle") and refers to a type of Buddhism prevalent in China and Tibet. "Ming chi" refers to tomb furnishings in China and derives from the word "*mingqi*," a compound of "*ming*" ("underworld") and "*qi*" ("utensil"). A "mei ping" is a Chinese porcelain vase with a narrow neck designed to hold a single spray of flowers. We also have a blend in the term "mafoo" applied to a Chinese groom, stable boy, or coachman. It comes from the Chinese "*ma*" ("horse") and "*fu*" ("servant").

Japan has provided a wealth of terms to describe the martial arts and sumo wrestling. We have the term "mae-geri," with "*mae*" meaning "front" or "forward" and "*geri*" meaning "kick." It is a front kick performed in karate by raising the knee of the kicking leg to waist height and then thrusting the extended leg forward to strike the target with the ball of the foot. A "makikomi," in judo and jiu-jitsu, is a throw in which one's opponent is wound around one's body before being thrown to the ground. Collec-tively, all the throwing techniques are referred to as "nagewaza." These words seem downright innocuous when compared to "ninjutsu," which is defined as the "Japanese art of stealth, camouflage, sabotage, and assassination, developed in feudal times for military espionage, but subsequently used in the training of warriors."

"Makunouchi" is a term used in sumo wrestling to designate the highest level of wrestlers and literally means "inside the curtains." A "maegashira" originally specified the highest rank of wrestler included in the opening section of a sumo tournament, but it has come to refer to the lower rank of wrestler within the Makunouchi division. An "oshi-dashi" in sumo is a winning move in which a wrestler pushes his opponent out of the ring; it blends "oshi" ("push out") with "dasu" ("put out"). The wrestlers are clad in a "mawashi" ("loincloth") and the word derives from "*mawasu*" ("to put round"). Washing the mawashi is said to bring bad luck, so it is dried in the sun but not washed.

Many new words are streaming into English from Africa, with a fair number of them coming out of South Africa and its environs. The term "madala" derives from the Zulu "*umadala*" ("old one"). It is frequently used as an affectionate, respectful address, especially to an elderly black man. The term "ntate" is also a respectful term for an older man and derives from the Sotho word "*ntate*" ("father"). The word "ouboet" derives from

Afrikaans and it is a term of endearment for an older brother or male friend. Not respectful, however, is the term "muntu," a derogatory term for a black African that derives from the Zulu "*umuntu*" ("human being"). The address "majita" is South African slang, and refers to a black youth or adult male. A female employer in South Africa might be called "nooi"; she would be the female equivalent to a "baas" ("boss").

Many of the entries reveal interesting snippets of African history. "Mardyker" is a historical term that refers to a "group of freed Malay slaves who were employed to fight for the Dutch colonists against the indigenous people of the Cape of Good Hope and also later against the British." "Ossewa Brandwag" is a revered symbol for Afrikaan nationalists and it means "ox-wagon," which was the means of transportation for the Voortrekkers, the original Dutch pioneers in South Africa. "Magwamba" refers to a people of the Northern Province of South Africa; "Magosian" relates to a Stone Age culture formerly thought to have existed in sub-Saharan Africa, from finds found at Magosi. The term "Mfecane" comes from Xhosa and refers to the dispersal of the northern Nguni people in the early 19th century to present-day Kwazulu Natal. "Mfengu" derives from a Xhosa word that means "to beg like a destitute person." It refers to Xhosa-speaking people who are descended from certain refugee groups during the Mfecane ("dispersal") who settled in the eastern Cape and Southern Transkei in the 1830s. We also see some new South African English adjectives emerging. "Makulu" means "impressive" and derives from the Zulu-based English pidgin Fanakalu, and "naar" means unpleasant and derives from Afrikaans and ultimately from Dutch.

The lexicon of music has been particularly enriched by the *OED* revisions. "Mbaqanga" is a style of jazz influenced by popular music, especially influenced by southern African forms. It originated in Johannesburg in the 1950s and derives from the Zulu word "*umbaqanga*" ("steamed maize bread"). The name of the musical style "mbube" derives from the Zulu "*imbube*" ("lion"). This word came from the title of a song first recorded in 1939. In a later rendition it was titled "*Wimoweh*," with the famous chorus, "The lion sleeps tonight." This style features male choral music and combines traditional Zulu songs with American gospel music. "Mgqashiyo" comes from Zulu and refers to a style of popular music featuring close-harmony singing (usually by a three- or four-woman group) of traditional or neo-traditional African songs set to mbaqanga rhythms and instrumentation. It derives from a Zulu word that means "to dance attractively or in a modern style." The word "malombo" derives from the Venda language spoken in South Africa and Zimbabwe. In Venda, it means "spirit" and refers to a rite of exorcism conducted by a diviner, accompanied by drumming, singing, and dancing, which elicits a state of excitement in its participants. The word also refers to a style of music that combines the drum style used in the Venda rite with elements taken from jazz and African popular music. At a malombo concert, one might be offered "majat," which the *OED* informs us is a term in South Africa for "marijuana, especially that of an inferior grade." At the same concert, a man may meet his future "makoti," which in the Bantu language community refers to a bride or a newly wed woman. Also out of the rhythms of Africa we have the word "mbalax." This comes from Wolof where it means "rhythm." In Senegal, it refers to a distinctive rhythm where all instruments are played in a percussive style. In Central and East Africa, a "nanga" refers to a small, simple zither or harp, usually consisting of seven or eight strings strung across a trough-shaped wooden box. A "nyatiti" is a musical instrument with eight strings which resembles a lyre, traditionally played by the Luo people of Kenya. In the Luo language *nyatiti* means "harp."

"Magaliesberg" is a type of tobacco grown in the Magaliesberg area of the North West Province in South Africa; it was used originally as pipe tobacco. "Mafufunyana" in Zulu refers to a form of hysteria, often believed to be the result of possession by evil spirits. More controlled is "maffick," which means "to celebrate uproariously on an occasion of national celebration" and is named after the relief enjoyed by the British garrison besieged at Mafeking, South Africa, in 1900. "Morabaraba" refers to a traditional strategic game, played chiefly in Botswana, where stones are placed and moved on rows of small holes in the ground, or on lines on a board. The object of this game is to capture all of one's opponent's pieces. You would be excused for thinking that a "middelmannetjie" referred to a merchant but it actually refers to a ridge formed between wheel ruts in an unsurfaced road or farm track. In Afrikaans, it literally means "little man in the middle."

We also find new words proliferating in other African locations. In East Africa, a "machila" is a conveyance consisting of a hammock slung between two poles. You don't want to confuse a "mzee" with a "mzungu" in East Africa. The former is a term of respect for an older person; the latter refers to a European or any white person. If you're in Kenya, you might take a "matatu," an unlicensed taxi or minibus. The word comes from Swahili and is a shortening of "*mapeni matatu*," which literally means "thirty cents" because in the early 1960s a flat rate of thirty cents was charged for a ride in this conveyance. If you travel to Tanzania, perhaps you will meet a "Ndugu"; the word means "comrade" and derives from Swahili where it literally means "relative of the same generation as oneself."

Many new words are also streaming in from the Islamic world. I mentioned above that the war against terrorism has given the term "mujahadin," fundamentalist Islamic freedom fighters, a much higher profile. The *OED* is also documenting other new terms in this region, particularly of Arabic origin, that are not as likely to be known by many people. The term "mutawwa" can refer to one who offers his services for the general good, but it also is also the name of the religious police in Saudi Arabia, whose non-too-modest official title is "The Committee for Propagating Virtue and Suppressing Evil." "Mukhabarat" in several Arab countries is the term used for the secret police and the term comes from the Arabic "*qalam al-mukabarat*" ("intelligence bureau"). A story in the November 14, 2005 *New York Times* said, "The mukhabarat is one of the most powerful and ubiquitous forces in the Arab world." The article quoted Sameer al-Qudah, a Jordanian, who stated, "We are hungry for freedoms like the right to express ourselves, but our country lives under the fist of the mukhabarat."

"Namaz" and "maghrib" refer to the ritual prayers prescribed by Islam to be observed five times daily. In the Islamic sect of Sufism, the term "murshid" refers to a spiritual guide who initiates one into the mysteries of faith. Literally, in Arabic, the word means "a person who gives right guidance." A "marabout" is a Muslim holy man or mystic, especially in northwestern Africa, usually living apart as an ascetic, and a "mawla" is a non-Arab convert to Islam adopted into Arab society. A "Nusayri" is a member of a minority Shiite sect practising a form of Islam with gnostic and animist elements; the term derives from the founder of the sect, Muhammad Ibn Nusayr.

The term "masjid" is used in Muslim countries to refer to a large congregational mosque where Friday prayers are conducted. In it, one will find a "minbar," i.e., a pulpit from which a sermon is delivered. (Given the Islamic prohibition agianst consumption of alcohol, it would be wise not to misspell this word "minibar.") In a mosque, the "mihrab" refers to a niche in a wall that indicates the direction of Mecca.

In certain Shiite Muslim communities the term "mut'a" (or "mutaa") refers to a fixed-term marriage, usually of short duration. Literally, in Arabic, *"mut'a"* means "enjoyment." An article in January 2006 in the *Los Angeles Times* reported that " 'Mutaa,' a 1,400-year-old tradition alternatively known as pleasure marriage and temporary marriage, is regaining popularity among Iraq's majority Muslim population after decades of being outlawed by the Sunni regime of Saddam Hussein." While the non-Muslim world has become familiar with certain prescribed forms of modest dress for Muslim women such as the hijab and burqa, few will be familiar with the term "niqab," which is a veil worn by some Muslim women, covering all of the face and having two holes for the eyes. The term "mudhif" in Iraq, and specifically among the Marsh Arabs of southern Iraq, refers to a guesthouse or reception room. At the mudhif, you might want to try out your new "narghile." According to the *OED*, the term is used for all types of hookahs in Turkey and the former Ottoman Empire, but in Iran it is properly applied to a type designed for travelling, in which the receptacle for the water is actually made from, or to resemble, a coconut. Finally, "manzil" is the distance between two halting places for travellers and derives from Arabic where it means "stopping place" or "station."

Australia and New Zealand are providing many colourful new words. In Australia, one should not talk back to the "maluka." He or she is the person in charge, i.e., the boss. It comes from the Djingulu word *"marluga"* ("old man"). In Australian Aboriginal usage the term "murlonga" refers to a white man who sexually exploits Aboriginal women. The term "mabo" comes from one Koiki Mabo, the principal claimant in the case that led to recognition of Australian Aborigines' and Torres Strait Islanders' ancestral rights to land. An article in *Time* on October 25, 1999 said that Mabo "by insisting that the law recognize his traditional ownership of a few garden plots, helped secure land rights for indigenous people across Australia, and changed the way the nation sees its past." Also believed to be eponymous is the term "maginnis," a wrestling hold from which there is apparently no escape. Hence, to "put the maginnis" on someone is to immobilize or coerce them. The Maoris in days of yore would engage in the odd "muru." This action was a raid undertaken as a compensation or reprisal for an offence against the community. The word "mauri" comes from the Maori language where it means "life principle." In English, it has acquired a somewhat similar sense and refers to the essence of something. "Makutu" refers to sorcery or witchcraft and in Maori means "spell."

You will also discover new groups of people in Australia and New Zealand. A "Nyungar" or a "Nunga" is a member of an Aboriginal people native to southwestern Australia; the name derives from the aboriginal word "*nhangga*" ("person"). A "Moriori" is a member of the original Polynesian people of Chatham Island. A "marae" is a courtyard of a Maori meeting house, and "manuhiri" refers to a visitor to such a house; in extended use it is a guest, a stranger, or a non-Maori. A "mihanere" refers to a Maori convert to Christianity, particularly Protestantism.

Animals are also receiving some fanciful names Down Under and in New Zealand. The "magnificent spider" lives in Eastern Australia and is noted for making spindle-shaped egg sacs several inches long. Also we have the "magnetic termite," which builds mounds that are aligned north-south. The "magpie moth" of New Zealand is a white moth, patched with black and yellow spots. In New Zealand, a "matuhu" and a "matata" are types of songbirds, an "oi" is a seabird, a "moeriki" is an extinct form of rail and the "ngiru-ngiru" and "miromiro" are tomtits. A "nanto" is an aboriginal term for a horse and is a shortening of "*pindi nanto*," literally "European kangaroo," as "*pindi*" means "European" and "*nanto*" is a term for a male grey kangaroo.

11

The Future of Global English

In 1585, when the Earl of Leicester arrived by invitation in Holland, he was met by scholars who had never seen an English book before. Well, things have changed in the last four hundred years. The verdict is in. Notwithstanding there are three times as many native speakers of Chinese as native speakers of English, English has become the global language. Consider some of the data.

English has an official status in eighty-seven countries and territories, far more than any other language.

Worldwide, over 1.4 billion people live in countries where English has been used, one billion of them in India.

Eighty-three per cent of high-school students in the European Union are studying English.

Of the world's roughly 12,500 international organizations, 85 per cent make use of the English language, with one-third using English exclusively.

English is the working language of 98 per cent of German research physicists and 83 per cent of German research chemists. It is the official language of the European Central Bank, even though the bank is in Frankfurt and neither Britain nor any other predominantly English-speaking country is a member of the European Monetary Union.

English is used in somewhere between 60 to 85 per cent of the e-mails sent around the world.

English is now the language most widely taught as a second language in countries such as Brazil, China, Egypt, and Russia. English is emerging as the chief foreign language taught in schools, often displacing another language in the process. For example, English has replaced French as the chief foreign language taught in Algerian schools, even though Algeria is a former French colony.

Whenever we turn on the news to find out what's happening in Africa, Asia, the Balkans, or South America, locals are usually being interviewed in English. When Pope John Paul II visited the Middle East to retrace

Christ's footsteps, he addressed Christians, Jews, and Moslems not in Latin, Arabic, Hebrew, or his native Polish. He spoke in English.

But if you're an English-speaking monoglot smugly sitting back waiting for the whole world to converse with you in your language, it won't be quite that simple. We English-speakers may never be able to communicate fluently with everyone everywhere. If we want to exchange anything beyond rudimentary messages with many of our future fellow English-speakers around the globe, we may well need help from something other than English. We may be well advised to follow the global trend and become bilingual, if not multilingual.

In the United States, one out of six people speaks a language other than English in their homes. Ever-wider swaths of Florida, California, and the Southwest are heavily Spanish-speaking. Of the 2.4 million Chinese speakers in America, over 80 per cent prefer to speak Chinese at home.

Linguist David Graddol wrote on in an on-line forum that "the whole point of multilingual societies is that you really need to speak more than one language to participate fully. … The question is whether monolingual English-speaking Americans will in future need to learn to speak Spanish in order to fully participate fully in American society." The spread of English throughout Europe is nothing short of rampant. Graddol finds it ironic that "English—so long thought of as the language of monolingual culture—is now helping re-establish multilingualism as a societal norm."

However, historically, it is monolingualism that is the aberration. The concept probably became entrenched in Europe with the development of the modern nation state, which led inevitably to the marginalization and suppression of linguistic diversity within national borders.

Some people who envisage English domination of the planet often point to the pre-eminence afforded to the English language, which serves as a lingua franca on the Internet, but this too might be a temporary situation. The consensus among those who study these things is that Internet traffic in languages other than English will outstrip English-language traffic within the next few years.

But even if an American feels that he need not know more than American English on his own turf, he had better learn "other Englishes" when travelling abroad. A Malaysian refers to a sidewalk as a "five-foot way"; a South African might indulge in "skinder" instead of "gossip" and might attend the "bioscope" not the "cinema;" and a New Zealander might attend a "tangi," not a "funeral." When a New Zealander tells you to "hook your mutton," you've just been advised to clear out. In India, a "bandh" is a "labour strike" and a "godown" is a "warehouse." In Pakistan, a "freeship" is a "scholarship."

Speakers of the world's many Englishes can avoid misunderstanding by consciously avoiding a word or phrase that you suspect will not be understood by somebody outside your country. One needs to find a mode of expression that is easier to comprehend. To facilitate comprehension, one can alter one's pronunciation and grammar. David Crystal stresses that it is still too early to attempt any empirical prognostication of the form that World Standard Spoken English (WSSE) will take: "WSSE is still in its infancy. Indeed, it has hardly yet been born."

WSSE is still in a nascent form, and I hope that *Global Mother Tongue* has demonstrated the interconnected nature of most languages. While I hope that World Standard Spoken English flourishes and helps bring a divided world together, we must never forget that it is a world language only insofar as it expresses the richness inherent in its cultural diversity.

Bibliography

Allsopp, Richard. *Dictionary of Caribbean English Usage* (Oxford: Oxford University Press, 1996).

Anglo-Saxon Chronicles (London: Eyre & Spottiswoode, 1961).

Avis, Waler S., ed. *A Dictionary of Canadianisms on Historical Principles* (Toronto: Gage, 1967).

Ayto, John. *Dictionary of Word Origins* (New York: Arcade, 1990).

Barnhart, David and Allan Metcalf. *America in So Many Words* (Boston: Houghton Mifflin, 1997).

Baugh, Albert. *The History of the English Language* (New York: Appleton-Century-Crofts, 1957).

Blake, N.F. *Shakespeare's Language* (Basingstoke: Macmillan, 1981).

Berlitz, Charles. *Native Tongues* (New York: Grosset & Dunlap, 1982).

Blancpain, M. and A. Reboullet. *Une Langue, Le Français* (Paris: Hachette, 1976).

Brewer's Dictionary of Modern Phrase & Fable (London: Cassel, 2000).

Burgen, Stephen. *Your Mother's Tongue* (London: Indigo, 1996).

Canadian Oxford Dictionary (Toronto: Oxford University Press, 1998 and 2004).

Casselman, Bill. *Canadian Food Words* (Toronto: McArthur, 1998).

Chevillet, François. *Idéologies dans le monde anglo-saxon* (Grenoble: Université de Grenoble, 1998).

Claiborne, Robert. *Our Marvellous Native Tongue* (New York: Time Books, 1983).

_____. *The Roots of Language* (New York: Time Books, 1989).

Crystal, David. *Cambridge Encyclopedia of the English Language* (Cambridge: Cambridge University Press, 1995)

_____. *English as a Global Language* (Cambridge: Cambridge University Press, 1997).

_____. *The English Language* (London: Penguin, 1988).

_____. *The Stories of English* (New York: Overlook, 2004).

Defoe, Daniel. *Essay Upon Projects* (New York: AMS Press, 1999).

Fishman, J.A. *The Spread of English* (Rowley: Newbury House, 1977).

Flaitz, Jeffra. *The Ideology of English* (Berlin: Mouton de Gruyter, 1988).

Franklin, Michael. *Sir William Jones* (Cardiff: University of Wales Press, 1994).

Grimes, William. *Eating Your Words* (Oxford: Oxford University Press, 2004).

Hall, Robert. *Linguistics and Your Language* (New York: Doubleday, 1960).

Hendrickson, Robert. *Words and Phrase Origins* (New York: Facts On File, 1997).

Homer. *The Iliad* (London: Dalay, 1878).

Jewish Encyclopedia (New York: Funk and Wagnall, 1945).

Johnson, Samuel. *A Dictionary of the English Language* (New York: Pantheon Books, 1963).

King James Version of the Bible (Chicago: Hertel, 1948).

Kipling, Rudyard. *Tales from the Hills* (Garden City: Doubleday, 1924).

The Koran (Harmondsworth: Penguin, 1983).

Lass, Roger. *The Shape of English* (London: Dent, 1987).

Lederer, Richard. *The Miracle of Language* (New York: Simon and Schuster, 1991).

Liberman, Anatoly. *Word Origins* (Oxford: Oxford University Press, 2005).

McArthur, Tom. *The English Languages* (Cambridge: Canto, 1998).

_____. *The Oxford Companion to the English Language* (Oxford: Oxford University Press, 1992).

_____. *Oxford Guide to World English* (Oxford: Oxford University Press, 2002).

McCrum R. W. Cran, and R. MacNeil. *The Story of English* (London: Faber and Faber, 1986).

Mulcaster, Richard. *Elementarie* (Oxford: Clarendon Press, 1925).

Orkin, Mark. *Canajun, Eh?* (Don Mills: General Publishing, 1977).

Oxford Companion to the Bible (Oxford: Oxford University Press, 1993).

Oxford Dictionary of Word Histories (Oxford, Oxford University Press, 2002).

Oxford English Dictionary (OED) Online (Oxford: Oxford University Press, 2000-2005). http://www.oed.com.

Pettie George. *Pallace of Pettie* (London: Chatto and Windus, 1908).

Pinker, Steven. *The Language Instinct* (New York: Morrow, 1994).

Pyles, Thomas. *The Origins and Development of the English Language* (New York: Harcourt, 1982).

Rivarol, Antoine. *Discours sur l'universalité de la langue française* (Paris: Delagrave, 1929).

Robertson, D. *A History of the French Academy* (London: Unwin, 1910).

Room, Adrian. *Room's Classical Dictionary* (London: Routledge, 1983).

Rosten, Leo. *The New Joys of Yiddish* (New York: Crown, 2001).

Shakespeare, William. *Complete Works of William Shakespeare* (New York: Books, Inc., 1956).

Sheridan Thomas. *A Discourse Being Introductory to his Course of Lectures on Elocution* (Los Angeles: University of California, 1969).

Smitherman, Geneva. *Black Talk* (Boston: Houghton Mifflin, 1994).

Steinmetz, Sol. *Dictionary of Jewish Usage* (Oxford: Rowman and Littlefield, 2005).

Styron, William. *Sophie's Choice* (New York: Random House, 1976).

Swift, Jonathan. *A Proposal for Correcting, Improving and Ascertaining the*

English Tongue (Menston: Scholar Press, 1969).

Talmud (Atlanta: Scholar's Press, 1991).

Zangwill, Israel. *Children of the Ghetto* (Leicester: Leicester University Press, 1977).

Véhicule Press